Beckett's *Happy Days*

Samuel Beckett by Sidney Chafetz (1976)

Beckett's *Happy Days*
A Manuscript Study

S. E. Gontarski

The Ohio State University Press
Columbus

Copyright © 2017 by The Ohio State University.
All rights reserved.

Library of Congress Cataloging-in-Publication Data
Names: Gontarski, S. E., author.
Title: Beckett's Happy days : a manuscript study / S. E. Gontarski.
Description: Second edition. | Columbus : The Ohio State University Press, [2017] | Includes bibliographical references and index.
Identifiers: LCCN 2016049718 | ISBN 9780814254028 (pbk. ; alk. paper) | ISBN 0814254020 (pbk. ; alk. paper)
Subjects: LCSH: Beckett, Samuel, 1906–1989. Happy days. | Beckett, Samuel, 1906–1989—Manuscripts. | Manuscripts, English.
Classification: LCC PR6003.E282 H4337 2017 | DDC 822/.912—dc23
LC record available at https://lccn.loc.gov/2016049718

Cover design by Susan Zucker

♾ The paper used in this publication meets the minimum requirements of the American National Standard for Information Sciences—Permanence of Paper for Printed Library Materials. ANSI Z39.48–1992.

9 8 7 6 5 4 3 2 1

For

Mom, Dad, John, Marsha and Jane—

the people who matter

most

Acknowledgments

This study would not have been possible without the collections of Beckett manuscripts at The Ohio State University and Reading University Libraries. I should like to acknowledge the generosity and cooperation of: the staffs of both libraries; Alan Schneider, Beckett's American director, who provided copies of his director's notebook and working script; Professor James Knowlson, Department of French, University of Reading, who made available copies of manuscript material from the University of Reading Library and from his personal collection, and who shared information freely; Samuel Beckett, who patiently answered questions and granted permission to publish excerpts from his unpublished manuscripts; Sidney Chafetz, who etched a portrait of Beckett for this study; and Professors Morris Beja, Gordon Grigsby, Richard Milum, William J. Sullivan, and Richard Weatherford who read portions of this study in manuscript. Their careful reading and helpful suggestions have made this a better essay. The blunders, however, are my own. Finally, I thank my research assistant Elaine McCarthy for her patience, and The Ohio State University Lima Campus Research Committee for its help with secretarial expenses.

All quotations are from the American editions of Beckett's work published by Grove Press, Inc. Quotations by permission of Grove Press, Inc.

Proust. All rights reserved, 1931; Grove Press, Inc., 1957.
More Pricks Than Kicks. Copyright © 1972 by Grove Press, Inc.
Murphy. Copyright © 1957 by Grove Press, Inc.
Watt. Copyright © 1959 by Grove Press, Inc.
Three Novels: Molloy, Malone Dies, The Unnamable. Copyright © 1955, 1956, 1958 by Grove Press, Inc.
Waiting for Godot. Copyright © 1954 by Grove Press, Inc.
Endgame. Copyright © 1958 by Grove Press, Inc.
Happy Days. Copyright © 1961 by Grove Press, Inc.

Contents

Acknowledgments viii

List of Illustrations x

Preface to the Second Edition xi

I.   Figurator 1

II. Primary Documents and Compositional History 7

III. Variations on a Still Point: *Happy Days* and
     Beckett's Persistent Themes 17

IV. Beckett's Dramatic Style: The Vaguening of
     Happy Days 33

V.   Low Comedy and the Antidote to Pathos 47

VI. A New Mythological Reality: The Literary
     Allusions in *Happy Days* 59

Appendix A 75

Appendix B 76

Appendix C 78

Appendix D 79

Selected Bibliography 81

Index 86

List of Illustrations

1. Etching of Beckett by Sidney Chafetz (1976) — Frontispiece
2. Holograph page, *Happy Days* notebook — 34
3. Page from earliest Typescript — 35
4. Page from final Typescript — 64

Preface to the Second Edition
Samuel Beckett's *Happy Days*, Genetic Study, and Book History

This genetic study of Samuel Beckett's final two-act play, *Happy Days* (1961), his only two-act play written in English, developed through a stuttering scholarly process, an unplanned series of fortuitous gropings, stumblings, swerves, and accidents that led, finally, from a box of uncatalogued papers, bedoodled manuscripts, and typescripts stored in a cardboard box in the back room of the Rare Books and Manuscripts archive of The Ohio State University library—where, as a PhD candidate, I was spelunking for a thesis topic—to the publication of a monograph on Beckett's creative process, the first such research in the field of Beckett studies. What those unpublished manuscripts and typescripts highlight, to this day, is how intractably difficult Beckett's handwriting could be when he was writing in something of a white heat, and I was attempting to decipher, transcribe, and assess those scribbles. The current reissue of *Beckett's "Happy Days": A Manuscript Study*, then, comes at a timely moment not only in Beckett studies but also in the general growth in programs of book history and digital humanities and is thus not just a look back to origins, say, as significant and historical as that may be, but further traces an arc of research that developed over forty years as the Samuel Beckett archive at the University of Reading matured, as the fields of both genetic and textual research likewise grew, and as book history reemerged on a grand, international stage. In Beckett studies, archival research developed, in conjunction with growing collections of Beckett primary documents at the Universities of Reading and Texas, both complementing that at Ohio State, as a central critical methodology. In this regard, we can note that the most impressive activities of current Beckett studies are the long-term Beckett Digital Manuscript Project and the complementary Beckett Digital Library Project, both based at the University of Antwerp, which also hosts the Center for Manuscript Genetics and the Centre for Genetic Joyce Studies; the Beckett projects are directed by Professor Dirk van Hulle of the University of Antwerp and Dr. Mark Nixon of the University of Reading, the latter also Director of the Samuel Beckett Foundation and the Samuel Beckett Archive at Reading. The Beckett Digital Manuscript and Library Projects, then, take textual production, genetic study, and book history into the twenty-first century with their emphasis on electronic access and digital collation and thus dramatically visualize Beckett's intellectual sources and creative process. Such manuscript and genetic study, moreover, has been an annual feature of the Samuel Beckett Summer School at Trinity College, Dublin, since its inception in 2011. *Beckett's "Happy Days": A Manuscript Study* is, then, a fundamental, even seminal, part of that forty-year scholarly trajectory, and in its current paperback reissue the book becomes readily accessible to students and scholars alike. With such availability, the volume grows decidedly attractive for classroom adoption and for use by scholars working with primary documents within a critical climate more amenable to its subject and methodology than it enjoyed during its original issue.

The initial project quickly took on the character of an exercise in paleography, and it was fraught with a variety of other research roadblocks, not least of which was the issue of permissions to use and publish the results. In 1972, as I was intent on working with primary material, these Beckett documents appeared to have been untouched since the transaction that brought them to The Ohio State University in the mid-sixties, purchased, according to then-archivist, Robert Tibbetts, from Henry W. Wenning (1911–1987), a rare book dealer specializing in twentieth-century first editions (although the current library staff seems unable to trace that provenance or verify any transaction of transfer, even with the clues provided above[1]). In the midst of this morass of illegibility and so unintelligibility, I wrote, almost in desperation, to Beckett's American publisher, Grove Press, with a plea to pass along a letter to Beckett himself asking for some help deciphering what I saw in places as hieroglyphics. The press dutifully forwarded the letter, which Beckett answered promptly, including, to my astonishment, his home address on the envelope. That gesture not only helped validate this line of research with my committee but also began a long association not only with Beckett but with his American publisher, Grove Press, and its head, Barney Rosset.

By 30 March 1973, Beckett was not only answering my queries regularly as they arose during the research process but was also offering additional information, advising me that his *Regiebuch*, that is, his director's notebook, for *Glückliche Tage,* the *Happy Days* production he directed in German in 1971 at the Werkstatt of Berlin's famed Schiller-Theater, "is available for consultation in the Reading University Coll. [collection]. Application to Dr. James Knowlson, Dept of French, University of Reading." I wrote to one "Dr. James Knowlson" on 4 May 1973, requesting a photocopy of the forty-three sheets of Beckett's *Regiebuch,* which he agreed to send in a letter on 9 July. I sent, in exchange, a copy of Alan Schneider's notes and his annotated copy of the play that I had secured during an interview with the director at his Hastings-on-Hudson home, the receipt of which Jim acknowledged on 15 October. The *Regiebuch* copy, "a copy of the copy," as Jim pointed out, was sent out on 22 September, and I acknowledged receipt on 8 October, after which I wrote to Beckett to request permission to quote from it and other primary documents directly. Beckett answered on 20 October 1973: "You have my permission to quote from the *Happy Days* material at Reading." Two years later, after several summer research trips to what had grown into the University of Reading Samuel Beckett Archive, I wrote to Beckett on 7 October 1975 to say, "I would like to continue my manuscript study of your work. For this I need your permission again to use the material and to quote, as in the past sparingly, from the unpublished versions and notebooks." Beckett graciously agreed on this and, as it turned out, on many subsequent occasions as well, offering, finally, a blanket permission to use what I needed for my textual research.

Beckett's cooperation was essential since the textual research I was conducting ran counter to the prevailing methodology and thinking on primary document research and textual study in the 1970s when the field was dominated by descriptive bibliography, on the one hand, and the production of heavily annotated, "definitive," or at least corrected editions, on the other—the latter spurred by the MLA initiative through its Center for Editions of American Authors (CEAA), which in turn became the MLA Committee on Scholarly Editions (CSE). The Ohio State University, particularly through the faculty of the Department of English and The Ohio State University Press, were then heavily invested in the CEAA project and were in the midst of producing the landmark *Centenary Edition of the Works of Nathaniel Hawthorne* published by The Ohio State University Press and edited and generally overseen by Ohio State Professor William Charvat and his collaborators Roy Harvey Pierce and Claude M. Simpson, with the assistance of a bevy of graduate students. The project was celebrated in a review for *Choice* as follows: "Because it represents the first scholarly effort to establish texts as close as possible to the intentions of the author, this Centenary Edition makes obsolete all previous editions, notorious for their textual corruption" (https://ohiostatepress.org/books/Book%20Pages/Hawthorne%20Centenary.htm).

My research, however, followed another path, one, let us say, that was less than popular at the time. I wanted to trace the author's creative process draft by draft, and to write a critical narrative, something approaching a biography of textual production, or what today is called genetic criticism, and not to collect and document textual variants on the way to establishing a standard, uniform edition, that is, my aim was to shift emphasis from distribution to production. For one, *Happy Days* was a mid-twentieth-century text with barely any distribution history no less one fraught with publication complexities, blunders, and other "textual corruption." My interest, then, was essentially *pre-* rather than *post*-publication, in the details of a work's genesis. I was most interested in the sorts of decisions Beckett made minute to minute, day to day, and they, I discovered, were evident or discernible in not only the textual changes but also in Beckett's notes and comments to himself. Fortuitously, it turned out that Beckett was a writer who did much of his thinking on paper, which material amounted, finally, to a conversation with himself. Beckett talked to himself in composition, and such conversation was not only a critical aide but would also become a major theme of both his prose and theater. Such a habit on Beckett's part and interest on mine would sustain my research at least through the end of the century.

I defended my dissertation in August of 1974, directed by Professor Gordon Grigsby, the year that Hawthorne's *Mosses from an Old Manse* was published as the tenth volume in the *Centenary Hawthorne Edition,* which series would then run for another thirteen volumes over the next twenty-three years. The two projects, however, could not have been much farther apart in philosophy and implementation. With the encouragement of and arrangements through then-Curator of Books and Manuscripts, Robert Tibbetts, my study appeared as the monograph *Beckett's "Happy Days": A Manuscript Study* from The Ohio State University Library Publications Committee in 1977. That library committee usually published, almost exclusively, exhibition catalogues and the like—and those essentially for local distribution—but my monograph on the *Happy Days* material held by Ohio State seemed equally central to the mission of Rare Books and Manuscripts.[2] The serious drawback to publication with the Library Publications Committee, however, was that the group had neither means of distribution nor budget for advertising, and so in those pre-internet, pre-website, pre-Amazon days, the volume languished, its existence noted in a flyer or two available in the library's lobby or in mailings to various friends of the library groups. Such limitations in distribution and access are more discernible in retrospect, but the book found a substantial scholarly usefulness—to judge by gauges like the citation index. The distribution issues are now ameliorated by the current reissue of the text by The Ohio State University Press itself into an entirely different critical climate, one not only more amenable to such genetic study but also to book history as well. More and more universities are developing programs that focus on textual production and histories of distribution—the development of the Columbia University Rare Books MA and the University of Virginia's Rare Book School, both developed by Terry Belanger, and the program I am affiliated with at Florida State University, the History of Textual Technologies (Hott) not least among them.

Some of the distribution issues might have been resolved early on by another fortuitous conjunction. Shortly after the *Happy Days* book appeared, I received a late night phone call from one Dougald McMillan of the University of North Carolina, Chapel Hill, whom I had never met but who was also working, as it turned out, on Beckett's theater through primary documents. McMillan had seen a review of the *Happy Days* book in *Choice* and was stunned, he acknowledged, that someone else was thinking as he was about primary document research and textual production. He asked if he might substantially reprint the *Happy Days* volume in its entirety in his forthcoming comprehensive study of Beckett in the theater to avoid his and his collaborator's (Martha Fehsenfeld) re-doing work already accomplished. I readily, even eagerly, consented, and that was the first of many late night phone conversations between us augmented by meetings, mostly in London and Paris, over the next twenty or so years, during which we discussed everything Beckettian—research, theories of scholarship, and particularly gossip—until his untimely death in 1999. Furthermore, James Knowlson was also seriously working on *Happy Days* primary material, and in a letter of 21 April 1976 he noted of his forthcoming, annotated, bilingual edition of *Happy Days*: "By the way, re. the edition, I have on the whole referred the reader to your forthcoming study for information on typescript development and holograph amendments [. . .]. You will see that I have acknowledged gratefully your own work in my afterword." Such references brought additional attention to the volume.

It was difficult to assess at the time, but, in retrospect, it seems clear that *Beckett's "Happy Days": A Manuscript Study* appeared in the midst of something like a golden age of Beckett studies with unprecedented levels of research, publication, collegiality, and bonhomie. Huge projects were coming along quickly, and those could not be passed up. Jim's letters were frequent and filled with possibilities. Jim thus was working on any number of projects similar to mine, although at that point his emphasis was more on production while mine remained focused on textual genesis, and we shared material freely without fears of encroachment. His comments in letters of 9 July and 22 September of 1973 established the ethics of our relationship: "We can then perhaps exchange information, acknowledged, needless to say, in anything we publish on the subject"; he reiterated that position shortly thereafter: "Help always acknowledged very gratefully in print at this end." Needless to say such arrangements were fully reciprocal. Jim's critical, bilingual edition of *Happy Days* would appear from Faber and Faber in 1978, and this project would lead to others. Jim would soon be editing the director's notebook Beckett kept for his 1979 direction of Billie Whitelaw in *Happy Days* at London's Royal Court Theatre, which again referred readers to the *Happy Days* manuscript study. Beckett was, at the time, in the midst of what had to have been a surprising new career as a theatrical director, albeit now exclusively of his own work. Jim, too, acknowledged the collegiality of the times in the published record of what was the first of the published theatrical notebooks, *"Happy Days": The Production Notebook of Samuel Beckett*, which appeared in 1985 simultaneously from Faber and Faber and Grove Press. In his formal acknowledgments, Jim thanked Beckett "firstly for agreeing to the publication of what was originally a private production notebook" (9), an acknowledgment we all shared, and, even as he was also able to attend many of Beckett's London rehearsals in 1979, he also generously credited and thanked Martha Fehsenfeld, "(who attended rehearsals on a more regular basis than I did) for her great generosity in allowing me to read and quote from her rehearsal diary and for providing me with the typescript of a chapter based on this from the forthcoming book, *Beckett at Work in the Theatre,* written by her with Dougald McMillan" (9). The book eventually appeared as *Beckett in the Theatre,* Volume I, from John Calder, a publisher in the UK, and simultaneously from his short-lived American publishing venture, Riverrun Press, in 1989, with Calder somehow misremembering and so misreporting its date of publication in the McMillan obituary he wrote for *The Independent,* citing it as having appeared over a decade earlier (see http://www.independent.co.uk/arts-entertainment/obituary-dougald-mcmillan-1128045.html). The Fehsenfeld production diary, which focused much more on Beckett's direction of and interactions with Whitelaw in rehearsals, naturally took precedence over the original plan to reprint my manuscript study in its entirety, but even then the study was liberally quoted. Thus while my *Happy Days* monograph was often cited and quoted in the Beckett discourse, the text itself remained elusive, almost inaccessible except by direct application and payment to The Ohio State University Library's Rare Books and Manuscripts division, a process all the more difficult and costly for European scholars and graduate students.

Somehow during this period of frenetic scholarly activity, as the inchoate field of Beckett studies was taking shape, I found myself conducting research, augmented by contact with Beckett, that was resonating with other scholars. I again relied on the Ohio State Beckett collection for the two *Endgame* chapters in what became a second volume of genetic studies, *The Intent of Undoing in Samuel Beckett's Dramatic Texts* (Bloomington: Indiana University Press, 1986). Furthermore, Jim and I went on to edit two volumes each of the uniform series, *The Theatrical Notebooks of Samuel Beckett,* Vols. I–IV, published jointly by Faber and Faber and Grove Press (1992–1999), my volume on *Endgame* produced in cooperation with, if not with the oversight of, Beckett who was still alive during the volume's preparation and was actively involved in the commentary and notes and in making final revisions to the text of the play.[3] The current reissue of *Beckett's "Happy Days": A Manuscript Study,* then, returns us to a point when such textual scholarship was still a nascent field but appears now at a timely moment not only in Beckett studies but also in a period of unprecedented growth in programs of material scholarship, book history, electronic editing, and digital humanities.

Endnotes

1. The *Happy Days* material is celebrated on the Rare Books and Manuscripts Facebook page augmented by a set of stunning facsimiles: https://www.facebook.com/media/set/?set=a.497028153646816.127078.200441529972148&type=1. Regrettably, acquisition history and scholarly productions generated by the collection—critical matters touching historical provenance broadly—go unmentioned in the overview of these Beckett holdings. Absent such details, the assessment of Beckett's work accompanying the images reflects a less sophisticated scholarly climate than now prevails.

2. See for example, Tibbetts, Robert A. (ed.). *The Compleat Bookman: Centennial Exhibition of the Work of Dard Hunter as Author, Papermaker, Artist, Typemaker, Printer.* Scott, Patricia (intro.). Columbus, Ohio: The Ohio State University Libraries, 1983.

3. These papers and my correspondence with Beckett are currently available at the Stanley E. Gontarski Samuel Beckett Collection at Trinity College, Dublin: https://www.tcd.ie/news_events/articles/trinity-announces-major-acquisition-of-samuel-beckett-papers/4571#.V1qSQiMrI10.

I
Figurator

The purposes of this study are to reconstruct as nearly as possible Samuel Beckett's composition of *Happy Days* and then to use that information to increase our understanding of the finished product. Furthermore, such genesis study gives us an opportunity to get acquainted with Beckett's creative process, a process especially significant for Beckett studies since the author's characters are often artists themselves, struggling with the problems of creativity. The reader or viewer eavesdrops on the creative process as he watches (or overhears) Hamm, the Unnamable, Henry, Mouth, Sam and Winnie write, revise, shape, and reshape their tales. And the creative struggle forms a major part of what passes for plot in the trilogy. Even Sam, who is ostensibly reporting Watt's tale (although it may be his own), cannot keep from tinkering with the narrative. Watt "told the beginning of his story, not first, but second, so not fourth, but third, now he told its end" (*Watt*, p. 215). Sam, however, tells Watt's story one, two, four, three. As Sam confesses, "I may . . . have left out some of the things that Watt told me, or foisted in others that Watt never told me" (*Watt*, p. 126).

Beckett's work also invites interest in manuscript and textual problems. In *Watt* Beckett, rather Sam, tantalizes us with breaks in his narrative: "MS illegible," "Hiatus in MS." Beckett rekindles in us an old hope of certain knowledge by obliquely suggesting that the manuscripts of *Watt* may reveal more than the printed text. If the critic could study the manuscripts, understand a bit more the author's creative process, fill in the hiatus, read through the ink blots, he might learn what-not (or what's what) about Watt and Knott. Even the indolent Murphy has a passing interest in textual problems as he ponders the possibility that Wordsworth's "fields of sleep" from "Intimations of Immortality" is simply a compositor's error for "fields of sheep" (*Murphy*, p. 100).

Beckett's analytical interest in the creative process is evident as early as his essay on Proust: ". . . the work of art is neither created nor chosen," Beckett suggests, "but discovered, uncovered, excavated, pre-existing within the artist, a law of his nature" (*Proust*, p. 64). Discovery of the "pre-existing" work of art, however, should not suggest ease of creation. Discovery, like conception, is merely the initial step; labor, of course, precedes birth. Beckett goes on in his essay to argue for Proust's distinction between artist and writer. Inspiration may initially impel an artist, but at that point, the artisan, the writer, takes over. "The artist has acquired his text: the artisan translates it. 'The duty and the task of a writer (not an artist, a writer) are those of a translator' " (*Proust*, p. 64). And translation is often an arduous, deliberate, and lengthy task.

Beckett's own process of composition is often complicated. The roots of many of his celebrated works, for example, reach back into early or discarded attempts. A number of works produced during the creative period (ca. 1946-1953) are, to one degree or another, derivative of earlier pieces. At the edge of the creative period, for instance, lie Beckett's first French novel, *Mercier et Camier* (ca. 1945 and which Beckett called a "dreadful book"), and the uncharacteristic drama *Eleuthéria* (ca. 1947, a play in three acts with seventeen characters). John Fletcher argues that both parts of *Molloy* are closely related to earlier works: Part I to the *Nouvelles* (especially "La Fin" published originally as "Suite" in *Les Tempes Modernes*, July, 1946); Part II to *Mercier et Camier*.[1] Colin Duckworth, in his study of the genesis of *En attendant Godot*, concludes that "the source of the dialogue between the boy and Vladimir is to be found in the unpublished play, *Eleuthéria*." He adds, "There are many coincidences of style and theme in *Mercier et Camier* and *Godot* . . . namely, the setting of the play; the origins and meaning of the tree; Godot; the rendezvous and the theme of waiting; the creation of the characters and the relationship between them . . . ."[2]

Lawrence Harvey traces parallels in imagery and theme between the unpublished *Dream of Fair to Middling Women* (ca. summer 1932) and two early published works, *More Pricks Than Kicks* (1934) and *Echo's Bones* (1937).[3] And Beckett himself has suggested to Colin Duckworth: "If you want to find the origin of *En attendant Godot*, look at *Murphy*."[4] The process of composition is complex. The artist may indeed discover and excavate the work of art from within himself, but the translation of that discovery onto paper and then into an acceptable, final form is, for Beckett at any rate, often a laborious task.

The hope of finding a simple key to Beckett's work in the manuscripts, however, is as futile as the wait for Godot. The manuscripts will not yield certitude no matter how hard we squint, but they can make us more aware of and consequently help us understand Beckett's creative process, something of his intent, and ultimately, the completed works. Knowing how an author works, or what sorts of additions, excisions, or alterations he makes, is a valuable aid to literary criticism. As Phillip Herring notes in his "Introduction" to *Joyce's 'Ulysses' Notesheets in the British Museum*, "the ultimate solution to many textual and critical problems is to be found in the manuscripts. . . . The study of an author's creative process can supplement many of the critical approaches to literature currently espoused by our graduate schools, since it forces one to look beyond the text, as it were, to discover how it arrived in its published form."[5] And of Beckett studies in particular, John Fletcher has noted:

> The way forward would seem to lie in . . . manuscript study. There exist now, at the University of Texas and elsewhere, collections of Beckett manuscripts, and Dr. Duckworth has shown the kind of thing we can expect from their close examination. If it is too much to hope that they will yield information about Beckett's intention and changes of mind as interesting as that made available for Flaubert by Mlle. Gabrielle Leleu and others, justice may well be done to some tenacious misconceptions, and a few tough critical nuts may successfully be cracked.[6]

J.D. O'Hara concurs: "Yet it seems probable that much future work on Beckett will be concerned primarily with the how, rather than the what."[7] While the unpublished versions of Beckett's work will not serve as a philosopher's stone, their study can improve our understanding of Beckett the writer as well as the completed works.

Happy Days premiered at the Cherry Lane Theater in New York on September 17, 1961, less than a year after work on it had begun. The play was shaped through a preliminary notebook and seven heavily-revised versions before it found its way to the printer and director. During the composition of the play both structure and content underwent substantial change. Tracing the play's growth through the early notebook and seven preliminary versions, the critic can follow Beckett's molding of the play from initial notes to the English printed and produced forms. By examining and comparing the patterns of revision, the excisions, additions, and alterations, the critic can follow the emphasis or de-emphasis on central motifs, shifts in tone, adjustments in dramatic style, and, in the case of *Happy Days* especially, the changing pattern of literary echoes and direct literary references.

The division of the play into the categories of tone, themes, style, and literary allusions is, of course, a critical convenience with some inherent dangers. The suggestion that each of the categories is a neat, separate unit is naturally a distortion of the unity of art, especially Beckett's. The result is some overlap in the discussion to avoid a rigid over-systematization. Defending Joyce's *Work in Progress* Beckett warns, "The danger is in the neatness of identifications. . . . Must we wring the neck of a certain system in order to stuff it into a contemporary pigeon-hole, or modify the dimensions of that pigeon-hole for the satisfaction of the analogy-mongers? Literary criticism is not book-keeping."[8] The danger against which Beckett warns is certainly real, especially when one severs too cleanly form from content. In *Work in Progress*, Beckett notes, they are one: "Here form *is* content, content *is* form. You complain that this stuff is not written in English. It is not written at all. It is not to be read—or rather it is not only to be read. It is to be looked at and listened to. His writing is not *about* something; *it is that something itself*.... When the sense is sleep, the words go to sleep .... When the sense is dancing, the words dance."[9] And Beckett praised Proust shortly thereafter because "he makes no attempt to dissociate form from content" (*Proust*, p. 67).

Since his vigorous (and at times, over-zealous) defense of Joyce's experiment, however, Beckett himself has insisted on the divisibility of *his* art, especially on distinctions between form and content. The inseparable union of the two can lead to a nonsensical imitative fallacy when the theme is the fundamental chaos of human experience (when the sense is chaos, the words are chaotic?); and Beckett is careful not to argue for the imitative fallacy. He acknowledges the need to shape human experience, "the mess":

> What I am saying does not mean that there will henceforth be no form in art. It only means that there will be new form, and that this form will be of such a type that it admits the chaos and does not try to say that the chaos is really something else. The form and the chaos remain separate. The latter is not reduced to the former. That is why the form itself becomes a preoccupation, because it exists as *a problem separate from the material* it accommodates. To find a form that accommodates the mess, that is the task of the artist now.[10] (Italics mine.)

Form, then, not matter or meaning, may be the primary concern of the artist, as Beckett revealed to Harold Hobson:

> I am interested in the shape of ideas even if I do not believe them. There is a wonderful sentence in Augustine... "Do not despair; one of the thieves was saved. Do not presume; one of the thieves was damned." That sentence has a wonderful shape. It is the shape that matters.[11]

J.D. O'Hara argues, therefore, that shape should be the concern of the critic: "In the long run, what is being said is of minor interest, while how it is said may make it last for centuries."[12] While Professor O'Hara tends to undervalue matter and overstate the schism, he does focus attention on what may be one of the less developed areas of Beckett studies, Beckett's shaping of the mess.

It is on form and process, then, the how, that the focus of the following discussion is maintained. The shaping of themes, tone, the pattern of literary allusions, and the overall structure of the play, ostensibly disparate categories, are all, fundamentally, matters of form—in Beckett's words, the translation of the original idea. As such, the line separating form and content is not always clear; form is to a great degree content, and a discussion of the one is necessarily a discussion of the other. The following essay follows the author's shaping the chaos, formally clarifying the mess.[13]

Before beginning, a word needs to be said about a standard problem of manuscript analysis, handwriting. Beckett's handwriting is occasionally difficult to read, especially in the heavily-revised, and consequently most important, early drafts which are filled with cancellations and additions crammed in. Ironically, Beckett dramatizes the transcriber's plight in *Happy Days* as Winnie, immobilized, hunched over and squinting, tries to read or guess at the words written on her toothbrush handle: "—(*examines handle, reads*)—pure . . . what? . . . . (*examines handle, reads*)—genuine . . . pure . . . what?—(*lays down brush*)—blind next . . . . (*examines handle of brush*)—slight headache sometimes—(*examines handle, reads*)—guaranteed . . . genuine . . . pure . . . what?—(*looks closer*)—genuine pure . . ." (10-11).

The difficulty of reading Beckett's handwriting has some effect on the completeness of the transcript. Illegible words are simply noted with an X. Other problems result from the difficulty of distinguishing individual characters in a word, or between upper and lower case letters. If a word is distinguishable but the spelling uncertain, it has been regularized in the transcript without notation. The pattern followed for capitalization is one established by Beckett. For proper nouns and words following terminal punctuation, upper case is used even when the case of the letter in manuscript is uncertain. When Beckett punctuates with dashes or ellipses, lower case letters are used. Aside from these emendations, the transcript follows the holograph as faithfully as possible. The symbols used in the transcript are as follows:

[> . . .]	Word inserted above with caret
[≯ . . .]	Word inserted above without caret
<	Replaces
------	Legible word canceled by lining out
--X---	Illegible word canceled by lining out
[. . .?]	Word or letter is conjectured
[→]	Addition made in margin, brought into text
[1]	Corresponding bracketed number on verso fits here
[X]	Illegible word.

References

1. John Fletcher, *The Novels of Samuel Beckett* (New York: Barnes & Noble, Inc., 1970), p. 129.

2. Colin Duckworth, "The Making of *Godot*," *Casebook on 'Waiting for Godot,'* ed. Ruby Cohn, (New York: Grove Press, Inc., 1967), p. 89-92. This is an abbreviated version of Duckworth's introductory essay to his edition of *En attendant Godot* (London: George G. Harrap and Co., 1966).

3. Lawrence E. Harvey, *Samuel Beckett Poet & Critic* (Princeton, N.J.: Princeton University Press, 1970), p. 254.

4. Duckworth, p. 89.

5. Phillip F. Herring, ed., *Joyce's 'Ulysses' Notesheets in the British Museum* (Charlottesville: University Press of Virginia, 1972), p. 2.

6. John Fletcher, "The Arrival of *Godot*," *The Modern Language Review*, 64, No. 1 (January 1969), 37.

7. J. D. O'Hara, "Introduction," *Twentieth Century Interpretations of 'Molloy, Malone Dies, The Unnamable'* (Englewood Cliffs, N. J.: Prentice-Hall, 1970), p. 25.

8. Samuel Beckett, "Dante . . . Bruno . Vico . . Joyce," *Our Exagmination Round His Factification for Incamination of Work in Progress* (London: Faber and Faber, 1929), pp. 3-4.

9. *Ibid.*, p. 14.

10. Tom F. Driver, "Beckett By The Madeleine," *Columbia University Forum*, 4, No. 3 (Summer 1961), 23.

11. Harold Hobson, "Samuel Beckett: Dramatist of the Year," *International Theatre Annual, No. 1* (New York: The Citadel Press, 1956), p. 153.

12. J. D. O'Hara.

13. See also H. Porter Abbott's interesting analysis of imitative form in Beckett's fiction in *The Fiction of Samuel Beckett: Form and Effect* (Berkeley: University of California Press, 1973).

II
Primary Documents and Compositional History

To date, the primary documents available for *Happy Days* provide the most complete compositional record of any major Beckett work: a preliminary notebook which contains an early fragment, and seven full versions of the play (three holograph, four typescript). In addition, documents relating to two significant productions are also available: the annotated typescript Alan Schneider used for his direction of the world premiere of *Happy Days*, and Beckett's directorial notebook for the German production, *Glückliche Tage*, which opened at the Schiller Theatre, Werkstatt, September 17, 1971 (ten years to the day after the New York world premiere).[1]

Beckett's earliest draft of *Happy Days* was written in a hard-bound, graph-paper notebook[2] now on deposit at the University of Reading, Reading, England. The notebook measures 21.7 x 13.3 cm (exterior measurement), and across the fading gray cover Beckett has written, *ETE 56*. The notebook is inscribed on the inside front cover as follows: "For Reading University Library, Sam Beckett." Facing the inscription, on the recto of the gray endpaper, Beckett has jotted down a partial table of contents:

Fin de partie	Scraps
All That Fall	
Krapp	First draft
Pim	Notes
Willie • Winnie	Notes

(In the notebook, but not included in the table of contents are also early notes for "Words and Music," dated February 16, 1961.) The 96 leaves of the *ETE 56* notebook are sewn together in six gatherings:

coll: (21.5 x 13 cm): [unsigned 1-6^{16}].

The *Happy Days* section, headed "[X] *Female Solo*," and dated Ussy, October 8, 1960, is twenty pages long, paginated in the recto of each leaf, 36-45. The fragment of text begins with the set description and ends with Winnie's mention of her occasional mild migraines. From the first, this holograph fragment reveals Beckett's emphasis on austerity—the "severe symmetry" of the set, Winnie's burial, and her morning ritual. After four pages of script, and in a flurry of changes about Willie's position at rise and Winnie's waking him, the first version stops, and Beckett uses the notebook thereafter for notes and tentative ideas, some of which are included in subsequent versions, others of which are discarded. The text of the play itself was transferred to another notebook, the holograph now on deposit at The Ohio State University, and begun anew the same day.

Of the seven preliminary versions of *Happy Days* on deposit at The Ohio State University Library, three are in holograph, four in typescript. All three holograph versions are contained in a common student's notebook: 17 x 22 cm (exterior measurement), soft paper cover (now a faded green), the spine reinforced with a black cloth strip. In the upper-center of the front cover sits a drawing of a square-rigged sailing ship, 7 x 6 cm, and beneath it, the brand-name, *Corvette*. Above the ship Beckett has printed in ball point pen: *HAPPY DAYS / OCTOBER 60 – MAY 61*. Inside, the cover is supported by a heavy paper front-piece and end-piece, and the 142 leaves of coarse, unwatermarked graph-paper are sewn together in 12 gatherings:

 coll: (16½ x 22 cm): [unsigned 1-5^{12}], [unsigned 6^{10}], [unsigned 7-9^{12}], [unsigned 10^{10}], [unsigned 11^{12}], [unsigned 12^{14}].

The text of the play is written on the recto. The verso is reserved for notes, ideas to be included in the text, fragments of dialogue, and most conspicuously, doodles of gargoyles, animal mutations, and geometric designs. As such, the verso pages of this notebook are very much like the *ETE 56* notebook after Beckett stopped the first version. The notebook is unpaginated, but references quoted in this study assume the notebook is paginated with consecutive arabic numerals beginning with the first page written on, i.e., the verso of the first graph-paper leaf; so that with the exception of the recto of the first leaf, all the pages, blank and filled, are assumed to be numbered consecutively to the end of the text. The first version contains only a single act, which eventually becomes Act I of the printed version, and runs from pages 1-72. The second version, which Beckett calls *"REWRITE"* contains two acts, begins on page 74 and ends on page 158. The final holograph version, titled *"Happy Days / Rewriting II,"* begins on 160 and ends on 234. Pages 235-283 are blank.

The four typescripts are currently stored in a blue, manila "Wallet File" folder, bearing the imprint of the British stationer, Walter Gillett Ltd.,

Brighton. Across the top of the folder Beckett has printed, again in ball point, HAPPY DAYS. The paper on which the four versions are typed varies little in quality, weight and size, and is a standard sort of typing paper, usually, allowing some variation for age and wear, 21 x 27 cm. The first act of Typescript I contains two varieties of paper. The first 12 sheets are a coarse, yellowed paper with no watermark. The remaining five sheets are a fresh, clean, French typing paper bearing the watermark, *Parcheminé Guérimand Voiron* and a shamrock insignia. Act II of Typescript I and both acts of Typescript II are also typed on the *Parcheminé Guérimand Voiron* paper. Typescripts III and IV are on a heavier stock with the watermark, Extra Strength / A.R.M.

The first typescript is identified by the author's headnote, "Typescript I," and bears no designation of acts. There are 17 sheets of paper in what eventually becomes Act I, but the final page is numbered 18, the result of an error in pagination between pages 12 and 14: no sheet is marked 13.[3] Apparently, Beckett paused after typing page 12. The page is a few lines short of the 50 per page which Beckett averages, and the last line is incomplete, even though no paragraph break follows. A note at the bottom of page 12 suggests that Beckett paused to estimate the running time of the play: the note simply says, "30 minutes." (Similar estimates appear in the first typescript of *Fin de Partie*, the two-act version, where at the end of Act I, Beckett notes 75 minutes, and Act II, 35 minutes.) Page 14 begins on the *Parcheminé Guérimand Voiron* paper, and with a line which was first revised then excised at the bottom of page 12. Despite the irregularities, pages 14-18 are clearly part of this first typed version of Act I since this is the only typescript in which the characters do not yet have their final names. (See Appendix A.) On pages one through seven, the two characters are called B and W (Bee and Winnie); on eight through 18, the names have been changed to E and M (Edward and Mildred).

The first typed version of Act II is catalogued along with Act I as part of Typescript I, but the coupling of the two is misleading since Act II was typed much later than Act I and belongs to a different stage of the development of *Happy Days*. Act II was typed after the second holograph version was written, and contains the final names of the two charcters, Winnie and Willie. An error in pagination exists in this first typed version of Act II also: both the penultimate and ultimate pages are numbered six, but seven sheets comprise the act.

The second typescript is identified by Beckett's heading, "Typescript II," and contains two acts, both marked as such. There are no errors in pagination in this version, but curiously both acts are paginated separately: Act I, pp. 1-17; Act II, 1-7. The separate pagination provides a hint that Act II was typed before Act I, and hence immediately after the first typed version of Act II.

Typescript III is identified by the author in an abbreviated fashion, "T III," and is the first version in which both acts are paginated consecutively, 1-24, but unfortunately the opening page of Act II, page 18, is missing and apparently lost. The final typescript, "T IV," is the manuscript sent to the printer and contains a formal title page (HAPPY DAYS / A Play in 2 Acts / by / Samuel Beckett) and a separate sheet for the characters, in addition to the 28 pages of text. Unlike earlier typescripts, this final version contains few revisions, but does contain thirteen carefully written out literary quotations complete with author and title of the work cited.

The fact of eight versions of *Happy Days* does not itself give a complete indication of the number of stages in the play's composition. The early fragment and preliminary notes in the *ETE 56* notebook are often revised before inclusion into the body of the play. In the *Happy Days* Notebook, key passages are written and rewritten on the verso before inclusion into the text. Each version, holograph and typescript, is also revised a number of times with, similar to Joyce's cancellations with different color pencils in the *Ulysses* Notesheets, a distinguishably different writing instrument. Finally, because of the apparent uncertainty about the number of acts the play would have, the eight manuscript versions actually represent nine stages of development. Using the manuscript revisions as evidence, one can establish the following order of composition (manuscript references hereafter as in parentheses):

Stage 1: Incomplete holograph and general notes; begun October 8, 1960, no final date.

(*ETE 56*)

Stage 2: First full holograph version, Act I only; begun October 8, 1960, completed January 14, 1961.

(H-1)

Stage 3: First typescript, Act I only; n.d.

(TS.-1, Act I)

Stage 4: Second holograph version, Acts I and II; Act I, January 16 - January 20, 1961; Act II, February 2 - February 7, 1961.

(H-2)

Stage 5: First typescript, Act II only; n.d.

(TS.-1, Act II)

Stage 6: Second typescript, Acts I and II; Act II probably typed before Act I; n.d.

(TS.-2)

Stage 7: Third holograph, Acts I and II; Act I, March 29 - May 12, 1961; Act II, May 13 - May 14, 1961.

(H-3)

Stage 8: Third typescript, Acts I and II; n.d.

(TS.-3)

Stage 9: Fourth typescript, Acts I and II; n.d.

(TS.- 4)

Happy Days then was first designed or conceived as a one- act play. Three versions of Act I were completed before work on Act II was begun. The first typed version of Act II incorporates the revision of Act II of H-2 into the text, so that TS.-1, Act II was clearly prepared after the H-2 version. Moreover, none of the three early drafts bears any indication that it is the first of two acts. And finally, although Beckett wrote steadily, finishing the complete one-act version in just over three months, typing that version in one day (between the completion of H-1, January 14, 1961, and the beginning of H-2, January 16), and then immediately beginning H-2, an uncharacteristic break of eleven days exists between the completion of Act I and the beginning of Act II of H-2. This is the only time during the composition of the play where a break of any length is apparent.

If the reason for the eleven-day delay was a structural crisis, it was not the first time Beckett was plagued with such difficulty. The composition of *Watt*, for example, presented problems. Although the bulk of the revisions in the *Watt* manuscripts are stylistic, Beckett apparently had some trouble with the original opening section which was first discarded and then incorporated into the addenda. Beckett also had a major structural problem with *Endgame*. Among the very few letters of his Beckett allowed to be published are fragments of the author's correspondence with his American director, Alan Schneider, printed in the *Village Voice*, and permission to publish even these excerpts was given reluctantly by Beckett. The letters are, however, enormously revealing about the kind of structural problems Beckett had while composing *Endgame*. Dissatisfied with the play because of its instability (at the time it was a two-act play), Beckett wrote to Schneider on April 12, 1956, "I did finish another, but didn't like it. It has turned out a three-legged giraffe, to mention only the architectonics, and leaves me in doubt whether to take a leg off or add one on."[4] Evidently Beckett did not find the image of a two-legged giraffe upsetting, for the solution to the imbalance of *Endgame* was surgery; two acts became one as material was cut including an interesting burlesque scene in which Clov is dressed like a girl, and an ending where Clov is disguised as the boy. For *Happy Days*, the solution was to shape another limb, and on February 2, 1961, work on the prosthesis was begun. Once the decision was made, Beckett wrote three successive versions of Act II, one holograph and two typescripts, before returning to Act I.

One problem solved by a shift to a two-act structure was the placement of Winnie's song, her irrational (or non-rational) burst of joy. Toward the end of H-1, Beckett outlined the play's (or the act's) concluding action as follows:

> Some days (i.e., between waking and sleeping bells) much longer than others
>
> Edward emerges from hole "to have another read"
>
> his definition X X of "hog" as she puts back toothbrush
>
> all back in bag. Long pause. She takes off hat and puts in bag
>
> Her song
>
> Ed. "Wanted bright boy" (*Long pause. Curtain.*)
> (H-1, p. 65).

All the action in the outline is included in this first full version except the song. When the first holograph was typed out, again no reference was made to the song, but this typescript would most probably be a fair copy of the holograph. Revising the typescript (TS.-1, Act I), Beckett penciled in additional dialogue for Winnie to pray, and wrote a note at the end, "Sing yr. song, W." Having Winnie express a desire to sing, yet not be able to, would restate a familiar Beckett theme, the Cartesian disjunction between mind and body. Both acts of *Godot* end with such a disjunction:

> Vladimir: Well? Shall we go?
> Estragon: Yes, let's go.
> *They do not move.*

And we are never sure whether or not, at the close of *Endgame*, Clov can or does leave: "*Enter Clov, dressed for the road. Panama hat, tweed coat, raincoat over his arm, umbrella, bag. He halts by the door and stands there, impassive and motionless, his eyes fixed on Hamm, till the end.*"

Although Beckett apparently wanted *Happy Days* to end with a song, song was clearly inappropriate to the ending of the play as it now stood. The play would not be shaped to a pre-existing plan. Playwrighting is also not bookkeeping. After Willie's blunt definition of hog, and Winnie's returning the last of her objects to her bag, there is no reason for a burst of joy, even though, formally, it would balance Willie's earlier outburst. A second act grew. At the end, Willie is crawling toward Winnie. Misconstruing his intent, she bursts into song spontaneously. The mind does not control the body: "One cannot sing just to please someone . . . no, song must come from the heart . . ." (40). The two-act structure is then unified by contrast: Act I ends with Winnie's desire to sing, but her being unable to; Act II, with Winnie's spontaneous song. Beckett shapes his play from within.

Alan Schneider read a typescript of *Happy Days* while visiting Beckett in Paris, liked it, and offered to find an American producer for it. Schneider read an unfinished version, for he reports having made some suggestions for the final version. He recounts that when he first read the play, Beckett was undecided about the final title and about Winnie's song. Beckett offered four titles to Schneider: "Tender Mercies," "Many Mercies," "Great Mercies," and "Happy Days." Evidently he had already eliminated the two working titles in the *ETE 56* manuscript, "Female Solo" and "A Low Comedy." Schneider suggested "Happy Days," and Beckett obviously concurred. Beckett told James Knowlson that the title was at once a descriptive statement, a cheery toast, and a reference to the popular song. For the final song, Beckett was undecided between "When Irish Eyes are Smiling" and the Waltz Duet, "I Love You So," from *The Merry Widow*. Mr. Schneider, for better or worse, suggested the latter.

Schneider received his working script from Grove Press before the play was published, and was unsure whether his typescript was prepared by Beckett or the Grove staff. It was probably not prepared by Beckett, however. The format and pagination of Schneider's script differ drastically from all four of Beckett's typescripts. Act I of Schneider's script is paginated 1-2 to 1-31 (first page unpaginated); Act II, 2-1 to 2-16; in all, 48 pages to Beckett's 28 (TS.-4). None of the stage directions is underlined in Schneider's script, while in both holograph and typescript versions, Beckett meticulously underlined each stage direction. Moreover, Beckett's abbreviation "Do." is written out "ditto" throughout the director's copy. Finally, Schneider's copy originally contained a number of errors and omissions (subsequently corrected in pencil); Beckett simply prepares his typescripts too carefully to allow obvious errors, some of which alter the sense of a passage, to slip by in such an important final version.

Even if Schneider's script is not an original Beckett typescript, it remains a useful document for understanding the play because of the director's notes. There are not, of course, a great many directorial changes. A director does not tamper lightly with Beckett's script. Schneider himself feels a strong responsibility to the author's intention: "In all the Beckett plays I get credit and blame for following the author's intentions. Rightly or wrongly, I consider that to be my responsibility; if the intention is specifically stated, I try to follow it as specifically as it's stated."[5]

Schneider did suggest that Beckett make one change, however. During the toolshed reminiscence, Winnie recalls, in all the published versions, seeing "tangles of bast" hanging from the rafters. Schneider thought the reference to the herb was too esoteric, and suggested to Beckett that he change it. Beckett complied, in a fashion, and offered "raffia" instead. For the world premiere of *Happy Days*, Winnie recalled seeing "tangles of raffia," not "bast."

Schneider's script does not contain a great many notes. *Happy Days* is essentially a static play with only two actors, and the script contains few blocking notes. In fact, overall, the script is only lightly annotated, and most of the annotations are simply question marks. Nonetheless the script reveals some of the qualities of the original production and as such is a helpful ancillary document to the study of the play. First, the script reveals some stage business added to the original script (i.e., "try to sing," p. 1-25 and "use of gun," p. 1-28). Second, passages Schneider thought were especially important are starred. Finally, the script is divided into beats which reveal the points at which the director at any rate thought a shift in thought or tone occured. Hereafter, Schneider's script will be referred to as "Schneider's Notebook."

The second supporting document is a notebook which Beckett prepared for his direction of the German production of *Happy Days*, *Glückliche Tage*. Like the *ETE 56* and *Happy Days* notebooks, Beckett's directing notes are also written in a graph-paper notebook, 13.7 x 22.1 cm (exterior measurements). The notebook is red with a slightly water-warped, hard cover, across which Beckett has written, *Glückliche Tage*, Berlin, 71. Inside, the front piece is green and covered with white intertwined dolphins, under which is printed, "Made in France." The 86 leaves are collected in eight gatherings as follows:
 coll: (12.8 x 20.9 cm): [unsigned 1-3^{12}], [unsigned 4-5^{14}], [unsigned 6-8^{12}].

The bulk of the text appears on the recto sides of the pages. Most of the notes were evidently made before rehearsals; some are stated tentatively, others are corrected and revised, apparently during production, for after all directing is also not book-keeping. These additions and revisions are, for the most part, entered on the verso pages and keyed into the recto text with either arrows or numbers. Conspicuously absent from this notebook are the doodles and gargoyles which populate the *ETE 56* and *Happy Days* notebooks. Evidently the stress of directing is less than the original creative effort. Also, the handwriting throughout the notebook is clear and precise, Beckett's public hand. References to the play are in German, keyed to the German edition published by Suhrkamp (1968).

The 86 pages of the notebook are paginated as follows: 1-27, 27A, 27B, 28-85. The verso facing page one contains a table of contents, complete with page numbers for handy reference. The notebook is divided into the following categories: Bag, Willie, Bell, Turn to Wille, I, Eyes to Willie, II, Text with Action, In which Hand, Repetition Text, Interruption Text, Repetition Action, Variation Action, Interruption Action, Quotations, With Glasses and Without, Possible Cuts, *Unmuth Bricht Durch* (roughly: indignation breaks through), Smile, Sound, *Requisiten* (props).

The notebook is revealing in a number of ways. First, it re-confirms Beckett's artistic fastidiousness, his preoccupation with details and minutiae (and as such it stands in contrast to Schneider's Notebook). The "known contents" of Winnie's bag are detailed, including items which are never shown (i.e., her comb and brush), and a cryptic "miscellaneous" category is included. The number of times Willie speaks and the number of words he uses are carefully noted throughout: "In all 17 sentences 45 words." Willie's movement behind the mound, where he is not visible to the audience, is carefully diagrammed. Winnie's smiles and happy expressions are meticulously outlined: 31 smiles, 5 happy expressions.

Second, Beckett's breakdown of the play reveals its symmetrical structure. On page one, the first act is broken down into eight separate sections, the second act into four. Act I: 1. opening to "Old eyes"; 2. to the point where Willie fans himself visibly and Winnie takes up her magnifying glass; 3. Winnie's "Fully guaranteed" to Willie's "It"; 4. to end of laugh; 5. to Winnie's "No one. (*Smile off. Looks at parasol.*)"; 6. to Winnie's ". . . (*voice breaks, head down*) . . . things . . . so wonderful"; 7. to end of Shower-Cooker story and end of nail filing; 8. to end. Act II: 1. to Winnie's "And now?"; 2. from Winnie's "The face" to "Gently Winnie"; 3. to Winnie's "Sing your old song, Winnie"; 4. to end. Professor Cohn, whose divisions I follow here since Beckett's are in German, dismisses the breakdown: "These divisions are in no sense structural, but a matter of mechanical convenience for rehearsal purposes only."[6] But neither are they completely arbitrary. At the very least, Beckett's divisions reveal points at which the author-director thought shifts in the play occurred.

Finally, the notebook contains occasional philosophical and descriptive statements which explicitly reveal or reinforce some of the play's thematic concerns. The sense of decay permeates Beckett's description of the props. In speaking of Winnie's disintegration in Act II, the interruptions of her action and speech, her idea of time, Beckett comments: "Relate frequency of broken speech and action to discontinuity of time . . . . Her time experience incomprehensible transport from one inextricable present to the next, those past unremembered, those to come inconceivable" (*Regiebuch*, p. 62). Also, the stylized and repetitious description of action which Beckett calls for in the *Regiebuch* is not only a source of physical comedy for the play, but also a clue to the means of Winnie's adjustment to her environment—habit. While the *Regiebuch* is not a code-book to the play, it reveals, in places somewhat more concretely than the published version of the play itself, what Beckett had in mind, as well as the kind of changes he made looking at the play afresh after ten years. The notebook will be cited as *Regiebuch* throughout the text.

References

1. Both the earliest draft of *Happy Days* and Beckett's production notebook for *Glückliche Tage* were kindly made available, with permission of Samuel Beckett, by Professor James Knowlson of the University of Reading. Professor Knowlson has been a frequent and invaluable aid throughout this project. See also Professor Knowlson's description of these items in his catalogue of the Reading exhibition: *Samuel Beckett: an exhibition* (London: Turret Books, 1971). Alan Schneider's script, courtesy of Mr. Schneider.

2. Curiously, some of Joyce's *Ulysses* Notesheets are also written on graph-paper.

3. The fact that page 13 is missing is no doubt purely coincidental and no inference of triskaidekaphobia is warranted. *Murphy*, one may recall, has 13 chapters; there are 13 poems in *Echo's Bones and Other Precipitates*, 13 *Texts for Nothing*, and M is the 13th letter in the alphabet.

4. "Beckett's Letters on *Endgame:* Extracts from His Correspondence with Director Alan Schneider," *The Village Voice Reader* (New York: Doubleday and Company, Inc., 1962), pp. 182-186. Reprinted from *The Village Voice*, 19 March 1958, pp. 8, 15.

5. Alan Schneider, "Reality is not Enough," *Tulane Drama Review*, 9, No. 3 (1965), 129.

6. Ruby Cohn, "Beckett Directs *Happy Days*," *Performance*, 1, No. 2 (April 1972), 112.

III
Variations on a Still Point: *Happy Days* and Beckett's Persistent Themes

Space, time, habit, memory, stasis, and flux have been fundamental themes in Beckett's writing since his 1931 study of Proust. Curiously, the Proust essay reveals more about the author's preoccupations than the subject's, and as such provides an important point of departure for understanding the action and characterization in *Happy Days*. Winnie is one of Beckett's creatures of habit, and habit, Beckett and Proust argue, blocks self-realization and deadens awareness. "Habit," notes Beckett, "is a compromise effected between the individual and his environment, or between the individual and his own organic eccentricities, the guarantee of a dull inviolability. . . . Habit is the ballast that chains the dog to his vomit. Breathing is habit. Life is habit" (*Proust*, pp. 7-8). In *Happy Days* the cause of Winnie's burial is never explained, nor is her initial response to it. The play begins after she has settled, after her environment and predicament have become familiar: "That is what I find so wonderful . . . . The way man adapts himself . . . . To changing conditions" (35). Winnie adapts with the help of three habits: ritual, language, and hope. All three protect her from self-realization and self-awareness.

Winnie's adaptation depends on her distorting her circumstances and patterning her existence with every-day ritual, itself an attempt to impose order on chaos, the void, the mess. As such, her plight is not radically different from the artist's; both order the chaos, but one suspects to different ends: Beckett so that we might see it more clearly, Winnie to say that it is really something else and to avoid confronting the wilderness within. The suggestion of Winnie as artist is developed through her most repeated ritual, filing her nails: "What is one to do . . . . trim the nails if they are in need of trimming, these things tide one over" (24). Winnie's action echoes and parodies Stephen Dedalus's vision of the disinterested, indifferent artist, paring his fingernails, an image Beckett used most dramatically in "Act Without Words, I." Writing (art in general), we are reminded, tides one over.

Language itself can be little more than habitual repetition of learned sound. Winnie's prattling helps guarantee her insensitivity; language can be another insulation from self-realization. Ihab Hassan's observations on Beckett's language are here pertinent: "Beckett considers language a dead habit; his rhetoric cunningly demonstrates the point. Sentences end by denying the assertions with which they began. Questions receive further questions for an answer. Misunderstandings, contradictions, repetitions, and tautologies abound. The syntax is often the syntax of nonsense, the grammar of absurdity. And silence, literal silence, invades the interchanges between human beings."[1] The techniques Hassan describes are also those of *Happy Days*.

Also important to Winnie's habitual language is Willie, a comforting part of the environmental furniture. The delusion of communication comforts Winnie: ". . . just to know that in theory you can hear me even though in fact you don't is all I need, just to feel you there within earshot and conceivably on the *qui vive* is all I ask" (27). The fact that Willie occasionally makes sounds is more important to Winnie than what he says. In answer to her request for definition of the word "hog," for instance, Willie offers a gross image: "Castrated male swine . . . . Reared for slaughter." Winnie's response is dissociated from the content of Willie's definition: "Oh this *is* a happy day" (47). The fact that Willie may be revealing something about his own condition seems never to enter her mind.

The language she herself uses is also little more than noise. It is redolent with banalities, clichés, half-remembered literary quotations and misquotations. And the titular phrase, repeated ad nauseam throughout the play, is the most hollow of the banalities. Language generally in Beckett's world is not a means of conveying meaning, but a balm for the sores of existence. Words are opaque not transparent: "they form that impenetrable barrier . . . which forever keeps us from knowing who we are, what we are."[2] Language is a reflection of the impotence of mind.

Language has a definite function, however. It is a means of familiarizing the unknown, the cosmic void, a means of ordering and compartmentalizing phenomena. Richard Coe argues: "Give Mr X—that indefinable Other, that alien Self—a name, and we can enclose him in our orbit, assimilate him, make him ours, familiar, harmless, three dimensional . . . . Nothing is mysterious, or frightening, or hostile, provided that the words are there to 'explain.' "[3] Naming and the ability to enumerate possibilities in a situation are means of stability for Watt. But as words fail him, he fragments into incoherence. Words no longer order and familiarize Watt's world because he expects from them more than they can possibly provide. Winnie, on the other hand, never demands that words have meaning, nor that word and object be permanently and divinely one.

For Proust and Beckett, then, habit is a second nature which veils the first, the primary, the essential. " 'If Habit,' writes Proust, 'is a second nature, it keeps us in ignorance of the first . . . .' Our first nature . . . corresponding . . . to a deeper instinct than the mere animal instinct of self-preservation, is laid bare during . . . periods of abandonment" (*Proust*, p. 11). For Winnie periods of abandonment, conduits to her primary self, are rare. Through most of the play we see only the facade of her second nature, and the facade makes possible her "happy days."

Habit offers serenity and stability. Tension occurs when habit and dullness are threatened, when the second nature cracks. The dramatic pattern of *Happy Days* oscillates between maximum dullness (contentment) and the occasional realization of sorrow (suffering). "The fundamental duty of Habit," writes Beckett, ". . . consists in a perpetual adjustment and readjustment of our organic sensibility to the conditions of its worlds. Suffering represents the omission of that duty, whether through negligence or inefficiency, and boredom its adequate performance" (*Proust*, p. 16). The dramatic action in *Happy Days* moves between Suffering, "a window on the real," and Boredom, "the most tolerable because the most durable of humen evils." Each time Winnie's habits are disturbed, she is threatened with awareness. In Act I, the dramatic action barely moves away from anesthetized serenity. Her rituals and habits are threatened throughout the act, but only mildly. Did she brush and comb her hair? What exactly is a hog? Is the word "hair" singular or plural? And Winnie fears the disturbance of her ritual, a disturbance which would lead to a confrontation with the nothingness and force introspection: ". . . the fear so great, certain days, of finding oneself . . . left, with hours still to run, before the bell for sleep, and nothing more to *say*, nothing more to *do*, that the days go by, certain days go by, quite by, the bell goes, and little or nothing *said*, little or nothing *done* . . . . That is the danger . . . . To be guarded against" (35, italics mine). She is incapable of simply confronting the nothingness. Such a confrontation is as close as we come to heroic action in Beckett's world. The protagonist of "Act Without Words, I" is capable of denying the dictates of the outside force and asserting his total self. He is Camus' rebel who can resist and refuse to pursue the essence of life, water, even if that refusal insures his own destruction. His defiance contains a touch of victory. But Winnie is incapable of resistance: "what *could* I do, all day long, I mean between the bell for waking and the bell for sleep? . . . Simply gaze before me with compressed lips . . . . Not another word as long as I drew breath, nothing to break the silence of this place." But approaching the void, the wilderness, a confrontation with her Self, she recoils almost immediately. She needs relief and takes refuge in her appearance: "Save possibly, now and then, every now and then, a sigh into my looking glass" (21).

Fortunately for Winnie's serenity, she does not run out of things to say and things to do simultaneously. When she finds nothing to do, she can speak; when words fail, she finds things to do. "Fortunately I am in tongue again . . . . That is what I find so wonderful, my two lamps, when one goes out the other burns brighter" (36-37). Winnie avoids confronting her essential self by alternating between the habits of ritual and language.

The tension, pathos, and fear of Act II are the result of a major disturbance in Winnie's world. Willie is apparently gone. To combat the disruption, Winnie erects illusions to replace the missing environmental furniture. She needs someone to direct her words at to keep them from turning within. If Willie is not physically present, then, she will demand that he be anyway. "I say I used to think that I would learn to talk alone . . . . By that I mean to myself, the wilderness . . . . But no . . . . No no . . . . Ergo you are there . . . . Oh no doubt you are dead, like the others, no doubt you have died, or gone away and left me, like the others, it doesn't matter, you are there" (50).

Another threat to Winnie's adaptation and serenity is time itself, "that double-headed monster of damnation and salvation," (*Proust*, p. 1)—salvation because it is an instrument of death; damnation, because, in the form of the past, it is a permanent part of us and has altered us; memory seals time into our being and presents a threat if allowed to surface. "There is no escape from the hours and the days. Neither from to-morrow nor from yesterday. There is no escape from yesterday because yesterday has deformed us, or been deformed by us" (*Proust*, p. 2). Habit if not an escape is a means of evading time, especially that time locked into the Self. But memory is a constant, potential threat, "a clinical laboratory stocked with poison and remedy, stimulant and sedative" (*Proust*, p. 22). Beckett, following Proust, speaks of two sorts of memory, voluntary and involuntary. Winnie, like Proust, has a bad memory—or at least a bad voluntary memory—and she struggles with it throughout the play, trying to recall petty things voluntarily: literary quotations, the phrase on the toothbrush handle, people's names, the definition of hog. But her inability to recall information from memory poses no real threat to her serenity. She can simply dismiss the problem if it poses too great a threat. "What exactly is a hog? . . . A sow of course I know, but a hog . . . . Oh well what does it matter . . ." (19). And she never actively and deliberately tries to recall those events which led to her present predicament. Voluntary memory, that part of the past which Winnie can willfully recall, poses no great threat. As both Beckett and Proust have argued, it is inessential.

Involuntary memory, on the other hand, poses the serious threat. When habit is disturbed, involuntary memory crashes through: "It is only necessary for its (the individual's memory) surface to be broken by a date, by any temporal specification allowing us to measure the days that separate us from a menace—or a promise" (*Proust*, p. 5). Winnie's uncertainty about having brushed and combed her hair disturbs her habit and the result is an intrusion of involuntary memory: "(*Pause. She raises hand, frees a strand of hair from under hat, draws it towards eye, squints at it, lets it go, hand down.*) Golden you called it, that day, when the last guest was gone . . . to your golden . . . may it never . . . may it never . . . That day . . . What day? . . . What now?" (24). The Shower-Cooker memory is also involuntary. "There floats up—into my thoughts—a Mr Shower" (41). "Strange thing, time like this, drift up into the mind" (44). And it is Mr. Shower who asks the most pertinent and hence the most threatening questions: "What's she doing? . . . What's it meant to mean? . . . Why doesn't he dig her out?" (42-43). But Winnie keeps filing her nails through the episode. As her voice breaks, she quickly returns to her bag.

Act II is the more desperate act. It opens with a fissure, Winnie's failure to perform her full morning ritual. She speaks no prayer. With her ritual disturbed, she struggles for the remainder of the play to restore the stability and dullness of the opening Act, but the lapses of second nature are more frequent, and she is virtually bombarded with involuntary memories. The result is that Winnie approaches a realization of her condition (albeit temporarily): "The bell . . . . It hurts like a knife . . . . A gouge . . . . One cannot ignore it" (54). But she has another refuge, her story, an autobiography, but told in the safety of the "Not I" third person. With her autobiography Winnie withdraws into words.

Winnie has still another habit which helps her through her day: hope, and hope is another narcotic. The hope that Godot will come keeps Vladimir and Estragon from facing the reality of the human condition and seeing "themselves in the harsh light of fully conscious awareness."[4] As Vladimir suggests, ". . .habit is a great deadener." Winnie's sustaining hopes are first that day will end, and second that perhaps Willie will come live in front of the mound and that the two characters will be joined. The latter is a personal desire based on Winnie's memory of Willie's past affection. Both hopes, however, are as futile as the hope of Godot's arrival, for if we accept David Hesla's analysis, Godot is future time which by definition cannot exist in the present.[5] Godot defines hope. He is the carrot at the end of the stick, always out of reach. Winnie's hopes provide her with insulation from the reality of her condition and reveal her lack of awareness of the flux of human personality. The hope of Willie's moving in front of the mound was occasionally a sustaining desire for Winnie, but once it is apparently fulfilled, Winnie's attitude changes. Her tenderness disappears: "(*mondaine*). Well this is an unexpected pleasure! . . . Reminds me of the day you came whining for my hand . . . . I worship you, Winnie, be mine . . . . Life a mockery without Win . . . . What a get up, you do look a sight! . . . Where are the flowers? . . . That smile today . . . What's that on your neck, an anthrax?" (61). Winnie's apparent personality reversal is foreshadowed in *Proust*: "The aspirations of yesterday were valid for yesterday's ego, not for to-day's. We are disappointed at the nullity of what we are pleased to call attainment. But what is attainment? The identification of the subject with the object of his desire. The subject has died—and perhaps many times—on the way" (*Proust*, p. 3). When, by chance, we grasp the carrot at the end of the stick, we realize that we really wanted a radish.

A second hope sustains her throughout the play, the hope that day (or existence) will end. In sharp contrast to this hope is the changelessness of Winnie's circumstances, and the contrast provides much of the paradox and dramatic irony of the play. The play opens on an ironic note of changelessness as Winnie reveals more than she realizes with the phrases, "Another heavenly day," and "World without end Amen" (8). Heaven itself is a static, eternal condition. As Beckett notes in his Joyce essay, "Paradise [is] the static lifelessness of unrelieved immaculation." And certainly the opening image—Winnie buried up to above her waist—is one of Beckett's vivid and concrete images of stasis, immobility and hence changelessness.

We perceive, of course, surface change during the play. Winnie's attitude toward Willie alters, and she recognizes that the natural world itself has changed. To speak of days, at least days delineated by the regular rising and setting of the sun, is to speak in the "old style," for nature no longer functions as it did in the past. In Act II, Winnie is further immobilized, buried now up to her neck, but her essential condition has not significantly altered as the tree's having sprouted a few leaves in *Godot* has not essentially altered the predicament of Vladimir and Estragon. Death itself may be such a superficial change, for it may not affect the problems of consciousness, and perhaps, if we examine Beckett's *Play*, death does not even solve the individual's social agony. Winnie is waiting in a world which is running down. As in *Endgame*, things are running out for the protagonists. Willie is running out of Vaseline. Winnie is out of toothpaste, lipstick, and, like Hamm, pain killer or medicine. Her eyes are deteriorating; Hamm's have deteriorated. Even nature has almost stopped. Winnie: "Do you think the earth has lost its atmosphere, Willie?" (51). Clov: "There's no more nature" (*Endgame*, p. 11). The themes of cachexia and entropy run throughout *Godot*, *Endgame*, and *Happy Days*, and Beckett's description of the props used in his production of *Happy Days* reinforces the decay and deterioration. The toothbrush has few hairs. Only fragments of a label remain on the toothpaste. The medicine bottle too has a damaged label. Winnie's handkerchief, Willie's boater and newspaper are all yellowed. Winnie's necklace has more thread than pearls (*Regiebuch*, 82-83).

The conflict then seems paradoxical: change and no change simultaneously. These are as Winnie suggests, "difficulties . . . for the mind" (51). Winnie herself verbalizes the paradox, with little indication of its import: "To have been always what I am—and so changed from what I was . . . . I am the one, I say the one, then the other" (51). Within the superficial changes she observes, her elemental condition is unaltered. Even the increased heat is not significant. "With the sun blazing so much fiercer down, and hourly fiercer . . . . It is no hotter today than yesterday, it will be no hotter tomorrow than today . . ." (38). In *Murphy*, Wylie notes that changelessness might have advantages: "While one may not look forward to things getting any better, at least one need not fear their getting any worse. They will always be the same as they always were" (*Murphy*, 58). But in Beckett's world Wylie's view is excessively optimistic; it fails to consider the paradoxical cachexia.

Thematically, then, *Happy Days* is strikingly related to *Endgame*. Like Hamm and Clov, Winnie and Willie are complementary characters, opposites. Despite her partial burial, Winnie remains in the dignified vertical position, a thinking animal; Willie, a beast on all fours, leering over a pornographic postcard. In both plays words fail, that is, fail in their essential function as conveyors of real meaning and agents of communication, and the failure of words represents a failure of controlling order, a failure of God. "In the beginning was the Word, and the Word was with God, and the Word was God" (John, 1:1). In both plays an insect represents the possibility of continued life. Clov is bothered by a flea, and Hamm, the anti-Noah at one point, yells, "But humanity might start from there all over again" (*Endgame*, p. 33). Winnie is fascinated by an emmet carrying its eggs. Both Hamm and Winnie pass the time by telling thinly-disguised autobiographical stories, and both fantasize about being watched. Hamm—"All kinds of fantasies! That I'm being watched" (*Endgame*, p. 70). Winnie—"Someone is looking at me still . . . . Caring for me still" (49). As Clov prepares to leave Hamm, he is dressed with mild ostentation: "*Panama hat, tweed coat, raincoat over his arm, umbrella, bag*" (*Endgame*, p. 82). Clov, carrying Beckett's standard array of props, is like Willie, "dressed to kill." In both plays the distinction between day and night has ended. In *Endgame*, we find only gray. In *Happy Days*, blazing sun; night and its promised relief never come. In one of the earlier versions of *Endgame*, while the play was still in two acts, the second act opened with Hamm's ironic remark about the beauty of life. The scene was cut from the final version of the play, perhaps because Hamm, acutely aware of his condition, would simply be mouthing a heavy-handed irony. But Beckett apparently did not want to waste the scene, for it forms the core of *Happy Days*. A similar remark opens both acts of *Happy Days*, but with the important difference that Winnie is never aware of the irony. Thematically, the two plays explore the confluence of tragedy and comedy. Nell suggests one of *Endgame's* primary themes: "Nothing is funnier than unhappiness." In *Happy Days*, the confluence is seen from another angle: nothing is more painful (or tragic, or ironic) than happiness.

But perhaps the most significant parallel between the two plays is the paradoxical, absurd desire to end, coupled with the inability to end. Like Vladimir and Estragon, Winnie is waiting for Godot, her salvation, an end. "Finished," says Clov echoing what Beckett has called in *Murphy* "Christ's parthian shaft" (72), "it's finished, nearly finished, it must be nearly finished" (*Endgame*, p. 1). Part of the frustration of *Endgame* results from the agonizing possibility that the game will not end in a checkmate, but in a stalemate, with nothing accomplished, no change. The young boy may replace Clov who may replace Hamm who may move into the garbage can (as Watt moved from the ground floor to the first), but the essential agonies of existence remain unaltered. Change is a minor readjustment of objects in space, but it does not affect the essence of the objects. As in Murphy's chess game with Mr. Endon, where at the end of forty-three moves neither side has lost a piece (although Murphy has tried), and Mr. Endon is preparing to move his king into its original position, the possibility of accomplishing nothing after hours of play is omnipresent. The schizophrenic Mr. Endon refuses to allow Murphy the solace of *End*, but forces him *on*.

The most forceful image of the inability to end in *Endgame* is the reference to the grains of millet. "That old Greek," probably Zeno or Parmenides, demonstrates that the "movements and thoughts of a finite being in space and time are unrelated to, and incompatible with, the 'reality' of the Universe, since the essence of reality is infinity."[6] Transferring a heap of millet from one spot to another by moving half the original pile at a time is impossible in a finite world. "In an infinite universe, the heap could be completed; in a finite universe, never, for the nearer it gets to the totality, the slower it increases."[7] In fact, moving any of the grain may be impossible since to move the heap, one must first move half, before half, a quarter, before a quarter, an eighth, before an eighth, a sixteenth . . . infinity. The action is impossible to begin. Attaining the Unit by halves is impossible; i.e., $\frac{1}{2} + \frac{1}{4} + \frac{1}{8} + \frac{1}{16} + \frac{1}{32} \ldots$ never equal one. Another of the Eleatic paradoxes disproves motion; that is, change and motion are illusory. The proof suggests that an arrow in flight is actually at each instant of time at rest. Is motion then the sum of these still points? Motion is illusion as is the apparent change we see in Winnie's circumstances.

Zeno's paradoxes are particularly significant to *Endgame* when applied to the end of time. The closer we approach the end, the slower time moves, the more impossible the end becomes. "Moment upon moment," says Hamm, "pattering down, like the millet grains of . . ." (*Endgame*, p. 70). In *Happy Days*, Winnie is buried in the heap of millet, or half buried, at any rate. In the second act, half again of her remaining self is buried. She is being buried by moments, time, but she will never be completely buried. As such Winnie is the dramatic embodiment of the Unnamable's vision:

> . . . the question may be asked, off the record, why time doesn't pass, doesn't pass from you, why it piles up all about you, instant on instant, on all sides, deeper and deeper, thicker and thicker, your time, others' time, the time of the ancient dead and the dead yet unborn, why it buries you grain by grain neither dead nor alive, with no memory of anything, no hope of anything, no knowledge, no history and no prospects, buried under the

seconds, saying any old thing, your mouth full of sand, oh I know it's immaterial, time is one thing, I another, but the question may be asked, why time doesn't pass, just like that, off the record, en passant, to pass the time.

(Three Novels, pp. 541-542)

The apparent change we see between the acts of *Happy Days* is actually no change at all. As Winnie herself suggests about her own condition, "No better, no worse, no change" (13). The parasol, ostensibly destroyed in Act I, reappears in Act II: *"Bag and parasol as before."* In fact almost nothing has changed: *"Scene as before."* In Act II, Winnie approaches the realization of the impossibility to end: "There always remains something . . . . Of everything . . . . Some remains" (52). But she is again saved by her habitual use of language. She never fully understands the import of the words she uses. What remains, of course, is some part of being, the consciousness, the I, the *preceptere*. Winnie's case is not so strange. We are all being buried alive by time. Habit is Winnie's defense against the agony of consciousness and the impossibility of finishing. But Winnie never fully realizes her plight. That lack of awareness provides the play with its central dramatic irony; that is, the audience understands more about Winnie's plight than does Winnie, but it also deprives her of any tragic dimension. Awareness and recognition are crucial to tragedy. As Camus suggests of both Oedipus and Sisyphus, "Oedipus at the outset obeys fate without knowing it. But from the moment he knows, his tragedy begins."[8] And with that knowledge comes the possibility of victory. Winnie never knows. Habits protect her from knowing. And although the lack of knowledge makes her happiness possible and keeps her from being tragic, it also blocks her victory.

*   *   *

The visual image of immobility, Winnie buried up to above her waist, was present in Beckett's earliest notes for *Happy Days*. (In fact, the central situation in *Happy Days* is very like the Unnamable's vision of Malone: "There are no days here, but I use the expression. I see him from the waist up, he stops at the waist . . . " [*Three Novels*, p. 292].) But originally Willie (Tom at this point) was also part of the opening tableau. One of Beckett's first revisions was to eliminate Willie from the opening, a change consistent with Beckett's working, descriptive title, "female solo." The revision reveals Beckett's changing focus for the play; Beckett wanted the audience's attention on Winnie. The complementary nature of the two characters will not be as balanced in *Happy Days* as in earlier plays. Winnie's opening lines, which establish the primary dramatic irony of conflict between circumstance and attitude were at first simply, "Another glorious day" (*ETE 56*, p. 37), and two "Amens" after her silent prayer. Praise for the day, given her plight, would establish the central irony, but only on a single level. Beckett's revisions of this opening monologue reveal a masterful bit of dramaturgy since they amplify the theme of elemental stasis within apparent change, and increase the importance of the religious irony introduced with the silent prayers.

The revision of a single word altered the direction of the entire opening scene: "glorious" was revised to "heavenly." With that change, the complexity of Winnie's plight is increased with the introduction of another paradoxical contrast, the conflict between the traditional blissful notion of heaven and its potential horror, its changelessness, its blandness, its eternity. The day Winnie praises as heavenly is more like a day in hell, and Beckett's early revisions reinforce the hellish nature of the day and its contrast with the ideal which was established with the inclusion of a quotation from Milton's *Paradise Lost* about the "Holy Light." The Miltonic image conflicts with Winnie's observation, "blaze of hellish light" (11).

In revision, Beckett creates an increasingly hostile environment. The countryside is altered from "grassy expanse rising gently," to the final "expanse of scorched grass rising centre." The original lighting description is changed: "Strong sunlight" becomes "Blazing Light." As the hellishness of the environment and its association with the eternal stasis of heaven increase, the ironies intensify.

The horror of heavenly stasis is reinforced by two additional changes Beckett made in Winnie's opening speech. Rather than have Winnie's morning prayers totally inaudible, Beckett had her speak two fragments. As the play was nearing its final form (TS.-3), Beckett added the two fragments in the margin: "For Jesus Christ sake," and the more devastating reflection of the impossibility of termination, "World without end." Horror emerges from these relatively innocent prayers when one realizes, something Winnie never does, that the traditional Christian concept of an eternal heaven is exactly the opposite of what Beckett's characters, including Winnie, actually desire. Winnie wants an end, if only to the day, but heaven is perpetuation, endlessness, the opposite of eternal peace, sleep, unconsciousness, that "Belacqua bliss" Winnie so admires in Willie. Heaven is the perpetuation of that something which always remains, the consciousness, the soul, the I. We are faced, then, with the possibility that Winnie is already dead, the action of the play the imaginative projection of the persistent consciousness. Like Beckett's *Play*, *Happy Days* may be another realization of Malone's fear: "Then it will be all over with the Murphys, Merciers, Molloys, Morans and Malones, unless it goes on beyond the grave" (*Three Novels*, p. 236). This is heaven. Or Hell. Or Purgatory. These zones, like the states life and death, commingle.

But Winnie is Beckett's eternal optimist and believes, like Hamlet, that perhaps the hellish sun can help her end, destroy her flesh. Hamlet's problems would end, he believes, if his solid and sullied flesh would melt. Winnie dreams of a similar end: ". . . and wait for the day to come . . . the happy day to come when flesh melts at so many degrees . . ." (18). And again, for it is a profound hope: "Shall I myself not melt perhaps in the end, or burn, oh I do not mean necessarily burst into flames, no, just little by little be charred to a black cinder, all this . . . visible flesh" (38). The horror is in the "little by little," and even then perhaps her agony would not abate, for the hope is superficial, for the flesh. Something would remain. In *Endgame,* Hamm understands the impossibility of ending as Winnie never does. He can speak of the "last million last moments" *(Endgame,* p. 83). Winnie never realizes that being charred to a black cinder may not be an end. For the audience, her parasol is a reminder. It was consumed by flames in the first act, but appears unscarred in the second. Hamlet too perhaps misses the same irony when he fails to recognize that death was not an end for his father.

Fortunately for her, Winnie never hears her prayer. It is simply part of her morning ritual. She becomes an ironic victim by her own innocent unawareness. She moves on to brush her teeth. She inspects them and in the first typescript, Beckett added two other ironic, religious phrases, both of which have for Winnie lost their meaning: "*Good* Lord . . . *Good* God" (italics mine). The adjective is sinister in context, but Winnie is not bothered by incongruity because words have no meaning for her other than as sustaining sound. She is never bothered, as is Clov, by the failure of words. In a fit of temper Clov can shout, "I use the words you taught me. If they don't mean anything anymore, teach me others" *(Endgame,* p. 44).

The themes of stasis and changelessness are brilliantly emphasized with the addition of the second act. Despite the peculiarities of Act I, Act II is "as before." But Winnie is buried now up to her neck, and the opening visual image creates the initial impression of change. Yet the change is as superficial and circular as the apparent change in the book of *Ecclesiastes,* in which the sun dominates as an image as it does throughout *Happy Days*:

> The wind goeth toward the south, and turneth about unto the north; it whirleth about continually, and the wind returneth again according to his circuits. . . . The thing that hath been, it is that which shall be; and that which is done is that which shall be done: and there is no new thing under the sun.
> Is there anything whereof it may be said, See, this is new? it hath been already of old time, which was before us.
> (*Ecclesiastes* 1:6, 9-10)

Winnie echoes these lines: "Yes, something seems to have occurred, something has seemed to occur, and nothing has occurred, nothing at all, you are quite right, Willie . . . The sunshade will be there again tomorrow, beside me on this mound, to help me through the day . . . I take up this little glass, I shiver it on a stone . . . I throw it away . . . it will be in the bag again tomorrow, without a scratch, to help me through the day" (39). The stasis is further bolstered when Beckett added the phrase "no change" twice to Winnie's opening monologue.

The paradox of stasis and entropy which Beckett so carefully reinforced in his revisions of Winnie's opening monologue and then orchestrated throughout the entire play are fundamental to *Happy Days*. Stasis, cachexia, and entropy, form a hub from which other themes derive like spokes. Stasis and deterioration intensify Winnie's problems of adjustment and force her defensive response with a variety of habits. And habit itself is an effective protection of the self because of a Cartesian, or more exactly an Occasionalist, split between mind and body, two separate, unrelated systems. Man, or Woman, has very little control over his actions because the system of mind does not control (or even work in harmony with) the system of body. Winnie cannot put down her parasol even though holding it up serves no useful function and affords no relief. On the contrary, it increases pain and wearies the arm. The parasol is another of the inadequate tools with which man must try to work. Like the scissors in "Act Without Words, I," it is useless as a real aid. Yet Winnie cannot simply stop using it. "I am weary holding it up, and I cannot put it down. I am worse off with it up than with it down, and I cannot put it down.... Reason says, Put it down, Winnie, it is not helping you, put the thing down and get on with something else.... I cannot.... I cannot move" (36). Song also cannot emerge from the body simply because the mind wills it. Song, says Winnie, "must come from the heart" (40). The Cartesian theme is a variation of Murphy's plight:

> Thus Murphy felt himself split in two, a body and a mind. They had intercourse apparently, otherwise he could not have known that they had anything in common. But he felt his mind to be bodytight and did not understand through what channel the intercourse was effected nor how the two experiences came to overlap. He was satisfied that neither followed from the other. He neither thought a kick because he felt one nor felt a kick because he thought one.
> (*Murphy*, p. 109)

Alan Schneider in his off-Broadway production effectively emphasized the Cartesian dichotomy by adding to Beckett's script several attempts on Winnie's part to sing. No song emerged. The visual image of the Cartesian split is, of course, reinforced in the characters themselves. Willie, wallowing along the earth on all fours, often naked, is the physical side of man's nature, while Winnie is the intellectual, albeit limited and defective. Such a neat dichotomy may be an oversimplification of a complex relationship, but it does reveal the relationship of character development to a central philosophical premise. Like Words and Music in the play of the same name, and Voice and Music in "Cascando," Willie and Winnie are incompatible, portions of a self which cannot unite. The theme is voiced by Winnie, again without understanding: "I know it does not follow when two are gathered together . . . in this way . . . that because one sees the other the other sees the one . . . '' (28). The Biblical echo of "when two are gathered" is here a bitterly ironic statement of disjunction.

Despite her literary quotations, Winnie is not one of Beckett's thinkers. She never has the sort of self-awareness and insight which haunt Murphy, Watt, and the Unnamable. She does not, contrary to some arguments, grow through her experiences. Edith Kern for one, suggests that Winnie comes "to resemble Kierkegaard's 'knight of infinite resignation' who, convinced that there is no happiness and *knowing* the absurdity of existence, shares the humdrum life of his fellow citizens, but does so with that inner *freedom* that only his particular *awareness* can lend him."[9] (Italics mine.) But Professor Kern's inventive analysis would lead us to ignore much of the play's climax.

Paradoxically, as the play nears its end, Willie's role begins. Until the final scene we have seen Willie primarily through Winnie's consciousness, an interesting structural achievement in the drama. Such a subjective treatment of a character is unusual for the drama, which of all the literary genres is the most objective. But Beckett has always been expanding and destroying traditional forms, testing their limits, their breaking points. In drama and fiction Beckett has demonstrated new possibilities, altering those two genres permanently. Although *Happy Days* contains two characters, it is predominantly a "female solo." Almost all of our knowledge of Willie comes through Winnie, filtered through that same consciousness that has avoided seeing and understanding its own plight. The impression that Winnie provides of Willie is that he is reasonably content, in a sort of "Belacqua bliss." He sleeps, unaffected by the bell; he admires the models on the pornographic postcard; we are reminded that he is the brute beast that Winnie occasionally envies. But in the final scene, we find the contrary. Willie, "dressed to kill," makes a desperate attempt to attain the one symbol of ending that has been present throughout the play, and which Winnie failed to recognize as such, the revolver. We realize, perhaps for the first time, that Willie is also in torment and is desperately trying to end his own life, Winnie's, or both.

The key to the ending is Winnie's attitude towards Willie's struggle. Her attitude toward the gun throughout has been romantic and scientific. When she first pulls it from her bag, she gives this phallic symbol a kiss. She wonders about the intellectual problem it poses: why natural law has not pulled the heavy gun into the lower depths of the bag. It sits conspicuously on the mound throughout the play, a possible means of ending her agony. And although the gun as Beckett described it for his production is very old, decaying along with everything else, and probably would not work even if one of the characters tried to use it, Winnie, nonetheless, leaves its potential unexplored. And we are certain that she does not understand its possibilities nor the reason Willie is trying to attain it. Willie's quest only rekindles ideas of romance in her. She sings a sentimental waltz duet while Willie musters all his strength to end, a physical attempt that Winnie is never capable of. Willie struggles to end, and hence to "Win," and Winnie sings: "It's true, it's true, you love me so!" The two have not united. The day has not ended. We have moved in an incredibly symmetrical circle. Tomorrow, to speak in the old style, it will all begin again.

References

1. *The Literature of Silence: Henry Miller and Samuel Beckett* (New York: Alfred A. Knopf, 1967), p. 206.

2. Richard N. Coe, *Samuel Beckett* (New York: Grove Press, Inc., 1968), p. 11.

3. *Ibid.*, pp. 37, 40.

4. Martin Esslin, *The Theatre of the Absurd* (Garden City, New York: Doubleday and Company, Inc., 1961), p. 24.

5. *The Shape of Chaos: An Interpretation of the Art of Samuel Beckett* (Minneapolis: The University of Minnesota Press, 1971), p. 134.

6. Coe, p. 89.

7. *Ibid.*, p. 90.

8. Albert Camus, *The Myth of Sisyphus and Other Essays*, trans. by Justin O'Brien (New York: Vintage Books, 1955), p. 90.

9. Edith Kern, "Beckett's Knight of Infinite Resignation," *Yale French Studies*, 29 (Spring-Summer 1962), 56.

IV

Beckett's Dramatic Style: The Vaguening of *Happy Days*

The early drafts of *Happy Days* tend to be more "realistic" than the printed version. The major structural and thematic alterations in the manuscripts demonstrate not an evolution toward fuller explanation of character and situation, but the opposite, a development away from what Beckett has called, "the grotesque fallacy of a realistic art— 'that miserable statement of line and surface,' and the penny-a-line vulgarity of a literature of notations" (*Proust*, p. 57). The composition of *Happy Days* is almost a process of decomposition, a direction consistent with Beckett's professed aesthetic: "The artistic tendency is not expansive, but a contraction" (*Proust*, p. 47). As such, the development of *Happy Days* is virtually a microcosm of Beckett's overall artistic development: the pattern from *Godot* to "Breath," from *Murphy* to *The Lost Ones* is toward absence, whiteness, silence (themselves impossible ends for the artist). And in the drama even character names are used less and less frequently.

In the first five versions of *Happy Days*, Beckett repeatedly struggled with the physical description of the set. From the first, the play's setting remained that of the printed version, but Beckett originally tried to describe the dimensions of the mound more specifically. Beckett's earliest notes on the play (*ETE 56*) contain a set description which is virtually revision-free. But the first full version of the play (H-1) has three separate attempts to render the set description with mathematical precision, the most labored of which is as follows:

>   Grassy expanse rising gently
>   front to low mound
>   summit about 4' high.
>   The swell of the ground is
>   broken, on either side of

Holograph page, Happy Days notebook

Pause. She turns back front, resumes lips. B unfolds newspaper - hands invisible. Tops of fellow sheets appear on either side of his head. W finishes lips, puts back lipstick in bag, rummages in bag, takes out small com- -licated hat, raises it towards head, suspends gesture as B reads.
                                                                                 thousand
(reading). "Rocket strikes Pomona, seven hundred/missing." (Pause. B turns page. W resumes gesture of hat towards head, suspends it as B reads.) "Rocket strikes Man, one female lavatory attendant spared." (Pause. B turns page. W resumes gesture of hat towards head, suspends it as B reads.) "Rocket strikes Fire, eighty-three priests survive." (Pause. B turns page. W resumes gesture, sus- pends it as B reads.) "Opening for smart youth." (Pause. B turns page. W puts on hat rapidly, takes up mirror and inspects result. B reads.) "His Grace and Most Reverend Father in God Dr Charles Hunter, dead in bath."

Pause. W lowers mirror.

(tone of fervent reminiscence). Charley Hunter! (B turns page.) I close my eyes - (she takes off spectacles and closes them) - and am sitting on his knees again, in the back garden at   , under the horse-chestnut, I can- not have been much more than fifteen, he had just been elevated. (Pause. Rhapsodic.) Ah the fond memories that crowd upon one at the mere mention of a forgotten name! (Pause.) My first ball. (Long pause.) My second ball! (Long pause.) My first kiss! (Pause.) A Mr Johnston, or Johnson, very bushy moustache, I suppose that is what vanquished my scruples. Old enough to be my father in those days and indeed it later transpired my grandfather. He was eager I recall to put his tongue into my mouth (B turns page), but as I could see no particular point in that at the time I of course demurred and ultimately refused. (Pause.) All this took place in a toolshed if I am not greatly mistaken, though whose I cannot imagine. We had no toolshed and he certainly had no toolshed. I see the piles of pots and the tangles of bast hanging from the wall and the shadows deepening about the rafters as the long winter afternoon wore away. (Pause.) Ah the happy memories!

(reads). "Wanted bright boy."

Pause. B turns last page. W puts on spectacles. B begins to fold paper. W rummages in bag. B folds. W brings out a magnifying-glass. B finishes folding and begins to fan his face with folded paper - hands invisible. W takes up toothbrush and examines handle through glass.

Page from earliest Typescript

> the summit by two
> ledges, the lower about
> 2' from the ground, the
> upper about 1' below summit.
> The summit exactly in the
> centre and would effect one
> of severe symmetry.
>
> (H-1, p. 2)

By the second typescript, actually the fifth version of the play, Beckett has simplified the description somewhat: "Expanse of scorched grass rising front to low mound. The summit 4' high and at exact centre of rise, is a flattened area about 3' square. The slopes leading up to it on either side are identical in contour. Effect of strict symmetry" (TS.-2, p. 1). But evidently the description left Beckett dissatisfied, for it was canceled, and in the margin he jotted a telling comment which characterizes many of the major revisions in the *Happy Days* manuscripts. The note says simply, "Vaguen." The result is the abstracted final version: *"Expanse of scorched grass rising centre to low mound. Gentle slopes down to front and either side of stage. Back an abrupter fall to stage level. Maximum of simplicity and symmetry."* While the change in set description does not affect the structure or thematic details of the play, it does reveal a characteristic distrust of, or reluctance for, definite explanation and development. As Beckett revealed to Tom Driver, "The key word in my plays is 'perhaps.'"[1]

A pattern of revision tending toward greater ambiguity is evident in the manuscripts of a number of Beckett's works. One of the important observations Colin Duckworth makes about the *Godot* revisions is that the arrangement for Vladimir and Estragon to wait for Godot was not originally verbal, but written down, and by Godot himself. "For Godot to have written the words himself," Duckworth concludes, "he must have a physical reality; this obvious consequence led to the omission of the piece of paper. But we see from this first version something not entirely without significance, that Beckett originally envisaged the two characters to be waiting for a real reason."[2] In the final version, the reason, the reality of Godot, and the relationship of the two waiters to him are more ambiguous. Richard Admussen observed a similar pattern of dramatic composition in the manuscripts of *Play* where, he notes, "the dialogue moves from the concrete to the vague."[3]

Describing the *Happy Days* manuscripts for the 1971 Reading University exhibition on Samuel Beckett, Professor James Knowlson has noted, "the setting is made vaguer, whereas the figure of the woman (Winnie) is described in greater detail."[4] But the pattern of vaguening is more pervasive than Professor Knowlson suggests. While we do learn a bit more about Winnie's physical appearance in the first full holograph version (i.e., she is about fifty, not forty, and plump), and still more by the final version (i.e., "*blond for preference,... low bodice ... pearl necklet* "), the overall pattern of revision throughout the manuscripts reveals a tendency to excise realistic and concrete details and a movement toward more ambiguous conflicts.

One of the play's ambiguous scenes, for instance, occurs near the end as Willie, "dressed to kill," ascends the mound. As the scene developed, Beckett added some concrete dialogue for Winnie, but the specific diction was undercut by the retention of a vague verb and a revision which drives the entire scene toward greater ambiguity. The scene is worth some attention since it is characteristic of Beckett's dramatic style in *Happy Days*. Beckett's earliest note on Winnie's dialogue as Willie ascends the mound is simply: "She: Is it the revolver you are after, dear, or me" (*ETE 56*, p. 41). The next note is partly more specific, but introduces an ambiguity about the alternative to Winnie. Is she referring to the poet or to the brand name of the gun? "Is it a kiss you're looking for or Browning?" (H-1, p. 153). When the bit of dialogue is incorporated into the text a few pages later, the tendency away from mentioning the revolver begins: "Is it me you're after, Willie . . . or is it something else? (*Pause*.) Is it a kiss you're after, Willie . . . or is it Browning?" (H-2, p. 156). The final version appears in the first typed copy of Act II (TS.-1): "Is it me you're after, Willie . . . or is it something else? . . . (→Wd. you like to touch my face . . . again? [*Pause*]) Is it a kiss you're after, Willie . . . or is it something else?"

Although "touch" and "kiss" make the scene more concrete, the incident is dominated by the vague phrase which, with repetition, takes on a sinister air, "or something else?" The earliest choice Winnie posed was simply, "the revolver . . . or me." The retention of the vague verb "to be after" and the excision of the specific reference to the revolver, create ambiguity. Is Willie struggling toward Winnie, the revolver, or both? And to what end: to kiss or kill her?—or to end his own misery? Does the "something else" also suggest at least a faint ring of sexual desire in Winnie? Moreover, twice in the *ETE 56* notebook Beckett has noted the possibility that Winnie believes that Willie may be coming to dig her out: "End: Come to dig me out?" The increased ambiguity of Winnie's remarks is important to her characterization since it decreases her awareness of the object of Willie's quest. She may not even be aware that Willie is possibly struggling toward the gun. Notwithstanding the addition of some specific diction to this final scene, the overall pattern of revision is toward increased ambiguity and multiple possibility.

One of Beckett's major revisions alters the fundamental conflict of the entire play. In the first three versions of *Happy Days*, Winnie is awakened not by the piercing bell, which Beckett has called Winnie's enemy, but by an alarm clock which rings softly. With the clock, Winnie has more knowledge about the progress of the day than without it, knowledge which she could use to regulate and order her own activities, pace herself to avoid gaps in time with nothing to do, shape her day with a beginning, middle, and end. The alarm clock offered Winnie a guide to the possible relief from the trials of the day (day's end), a guide not usually afforded Beckett characters. Near the end of the first typescript (the play's third version), for instance, Winnie consults her alarm clock: "(*Pause. She takes up and consults clock.*) The day is now well advanced—according to this. Perhaps I should set it for bedtime, while I think of it. (*She sets and winds clock. As she does so.*) Otherwise one is liable to overshoot the hour. (*Winding.*) and there is not much point in that." But Beckett was evidently bothered by the alarm clock, even though he stipulated that the clock should face away from the audience. First, he moved the alarm clock into Winnie's bag (*ETE 56*, p. 40), then finally cut it altogether: "Cut out alarm-clock. Invisible bell" (*ETE 56*, p. 42).

The revision from alarm clock to piercing bell affects the shape and direction of the entire play; the essential conflict is altered and intensified. The tension and conflict in the earlier version depend on a variation of the Cartesian split between mind and body, on the counterpoint between Winnie's struggles to regulate her day and the futility of human action, where one is even powerless to doff one's hat: "to think there are times when one simply cannot take off one's hat, not if one's life were (→ at stake). Times when one cannot put it on, times when one cannot take it off" (TS.-1, p. 7). This earlier conflict is personal; the obligation for ordering the day is Winnie's. If the result is chaos, the failure is individual, a failure of self, and such individual failure is the basis of tragedy, classical tragedy at any rate. In revision, however, the play moves toward the pathetic, toward what Jan Kott calls the grotesque, as the self is more the helpless victim of a vague, outside force. The result is a conflict more cosmic, but less clearly defined since little is said specifically of the force directing Winnie. Like the protagonist in Beckett's first mime, "Act Without Words, 1," or the characters responding to the light inquisitor of *Play*, Winnie's struggle is with some loosely defined outside force which is not really God, nor nature, nor history, nor others. Unlike the protagonist of the mime, however, the Winnie of the final version does not have the quasi-heroic potential in her personality of refusing to play the game. While she regulated her action with the alarm clock, she retained a certain freedom of choice; she could conceivably choose not to respond to the gentle summons of the alarm, or she might simply switch it off and return to sleep. In the earlier drafts, the relationship between Winnie and the clock is clearly less hostile than between Winnie and the bell. "*Alarm rings loudly, runs down, stops. Neither has stirred. Thirty seconds. Alarm rings softly. Woman starts awake* "(*ETE 56*, p. 37). In revision the intensity of the summons is increased and the duration between summonses shortened. "*A bell rings piercingly, say ten seconds, stops. She does not move. Pause. Bell more piercingly, say five seconds. She wakes* " (8). Choice and what limited free will Winnie had were eliminated as the play developed. The bell is violent and demanding: "how often I have said, Ignore it, Winnie, ignore the bell, pay no heed, just sleep and wake, sleep and wake, as you please. . . . But no" (54). She can only comply with the demands of the grotesque, absurd force. As Jan Kott describes the grotesque, paltry man is pitted against the absolute, which "is not endowed with any ultimate reasons; it is stronger and that is all. The absolute is absurd."⁵

At the end of the final version of *Happy Days*, the conflict between Winnie and the blind mechanism is acute. Having finished her romantic love-song, she closes her eyes to end a perfect day, but the bell has the last jab: whatever serenity she was building towards is shattered when, "*Bell rings loudly.*" The final pain is crueler than tragedy, for it is punishment without justice, but it is the view of tragedy that Beckett expressed in his essay on Proust: "Tragedy is not concerned with human justice. Tragedy is the statement of an expiation, but not the miserable expiation of a codified breach of a local arrangement, organised by the knaves for the fools. The tragic figure represents the expiation of original sin, of the original and eternal sin of him and all his 'soci malorum,' the sin of having been born" (*Proust*, p. 49).

Cutting the alarm clock sequence destroys the possibility of Winnie's measuring the day's progress. Winnie is no longer sure when or if her day will end. With the clock she might know that day is not ending, that perhaps days no longer end. The knowledge might shatter her artificial yet carefully established serenity. The possibility of endlessness, a glimpse at the void, is precisely the vision which must be kept from her to maintain her character. Beckett decreases awareness and the possibility of ordering her day with ritual with another excision. An oversized shopping bag lies beside Winnie throughout the play. In it are various objects which help her pass the time when words fail. In the earlier drafts, she knew and could enumerate more of the bag's contents than in the later versions. The bag, as Beckett described it, is her friend, and when she knew more about the bag's contents, the possibilities of enduring the day were greater. In the second draft, she could say: "I could name many things of course, those I require daily, others of occasional utility, perhaps forty or fifty all told, but all, no, I could not name all . . . . No . . . . The deeper layers in particular, who knows what f̶o̶r̶g̶o̶t̶t̶e̶n̶ treasures—letters, favours, tokens, trinkets, petals, dance-cards with pencils, theatre and concert programmes. (*Pause. Break in voice.*) Prospectuses. (*Pause. Do.*) Buttons" (TS.-1, p.11). In the final version, the list is eliminated and with it an indication that time or days still pass, as they did in the "old style," and that her ritual varied. We are deprived of this residue of Winnie's life, dregs which provided details from Winnie's past. What remains in the final text is only a suggestion of additional objects hidden in the depths of her bag: " Could I, if some kind person were to come along and ask, What all have you got in that big black bag, Winnie? give an exhaustive answer? . . . . No . . . . The depths in particular, who knows what treasures . . . . What comforts" (32). Curiously, when Beckett prepared a list of the contents of Winnie's bag in his production *Regiebuch*, he divided them between the headings "known contents" (which included comb and brush, neither of which is shown in the play), and the rather mysterious "miscellaneous" category, also marked "not shown" (*Regiebuch*, p. 3). Winnie, with fewer known objects, is more alone and helpless, has fewer comforts; she has or knows of fewer objects with which to pass time. If the bag is Winnie's friend, as Beckett suggests, she now has less of a friend.

The second fundamental change is the decrease in Willie's role. Consequently, the knowledge he possesses about the present predicament is also eliminated. In the earlier versions of the play, Willie is still the reticent counterpoint to the loquacious Winnie, but he speaks more frequently and the extra tidbits he reads from the *Reynolds News* provide more concrete information about the couple's plight. In the final version, we have no idea why Willie can only crawl, why Winnie is buried—they simply are, examples of the modern human condition which is itself beyond explanation. But in the first two drafts of the play (H-1, TS.-1), the two characters appear to be part of an entire world gone mad. Both *Endgame* and *Happy Days* are permeated with the suggestion of nuclear devastation, and in the early versions of *Happy Days* Beckett himself suggests explicitly that Willie and Winnie are part of a larger technological world out of control. Willie, called simply "B" at this point, reads from his yellowed newspaper: " 'Rocket strikes Pomona, seven hundred thousand missing' . . . . 'Rocket strikes Man, one female lavatory attendant spared.' . . . (→ 'Aberrant rocket strikes Erin), eighty-three priests survive' " (TS.-1, p. 4). The seriousness of the devastation is undercut by the incongruous scatological and anti-clerical suggestions, but Beckett originally followed the horror with a brilliantly comic understatement: "Opening for smart youth." With seven hundred thousand missing one would expect at least several openings. The horrible blend of grotesque and comic must have been difficult to cut. Beckett's initial impulse was to expand the scene by having Winnie echo: "Sixty three priests, did you say? (*Pause.*) Was it 63 priests I heard you say, Edward?" Edward's response was typically curt: "83." But this note Beckett wrote to himself in the *ETE 56* notebook was never incorporated into the text, and Beckett finally cut the entire scene. If the section on technological insanity were allowed to stand, the focus of the play would broaden to include a world-wide madness, and the isolated examination of the couple might be lost. And perhaps the madness of modern technological existence and the arbitrariness of survival (a favorite Beckett theme) are too self-evident for Beckett to dramatize so blatantly. But even if the excision of the rocket attacks helps Beckett maintain the play's focus on his two specimens, a microscopic vision, and moves the play from a realistic to a more ethereal, metaphysical reality, it also suggests Beckett's preference (a preference which dominates his later work) for less clearly defined situations, a desire to move beyond the realistic, recognizable world. Beckett has praised the work of the painter Bram Van Velde because he was "the first to submit wholly to the incoercible absence of relation . . . ."[6] With the excision of the rocket attack, Beckett moves *Happy Days* further away from relation.

A realistic explanation of how Beckett's characters fell into their predicament may finally be irrelevant. They are there—born, on earth—and there is no cure for that. A realistic and accurate explanation of their past, if such were possible, is no help to them or us since the past is not something one uses to make sense of the present. Beckett's artistic aim is not to explain the mess or its causes: "The only chance of renovation is to open our eyes and see the mess. It is not a mess you can make sense of."[7]

The third set of revisions affects the level of Winnie's characterization. As Beckett reshaped the structure of *Happy Days* from one to two acts, two scenes which focus on Winnie's past and develop sympathy for her are cut. The cuts are consistent with the new tonal pattern established by Beckett for the two-act structure: Act I is predominantly comic, with serious revelation often undercut with comic action; pathos and desperation are reserved for Act II. The result is a second act more repetitious than *Godot's* since in *Happy Days* the major difference between the acts is tone. Once Beckett decided on a second act, he made a number of cuts in the original material to increase Winnie's comic detachment from the audience and ensure that, in the first act at least, she remains more caricature than character; with the cuts, however, some intimate information about Winnie's past and an emotional dramatization of her growing desperation are lost.

In the one-act version of *Happy Days*, the first holograph and typescript, the sexual overtones of both the Charlie Hunter (at one stage called Bunny Hunter) and Johnston reminiscences are more explicit. Winnie was originally confronted with sexual advances from a man old enough to be her grandfather: "A Mr Johnston, or Johnson, very bushy moustache, (→ very brown), I suppose that is what vanquished my scruples. Old enough to be my father in those days and indeed it later transpired my grandfather. He was eager I recall to put his tongue in my mouth" (TS.-1, p. 4). The original reminiscence has no interruption between the Johnston story and the Hunter story; given the sexual nature of the Johnston story, one suspects that the Most Reverend Hunter, not long ago elevated (a sexual pun Beckett evidently could not resist), with the fifteen-year-old Winnie sitting on his knee, may have had more than paternal affection for her. In revision, definition of the relationship is vaguened; the sexual advance and the mention of Johnston's age are cut; the connection of the two reminiscences is decreased by Willie's interruption, "Opening for smart youth." The sexual overtones of the final version are carried by the word "tool." As a result of the excision Winnie is less the victim of the men in her life and sympathy for her is decreased in the first act to maintain its comic tone.

The allusion to Winnie's youthful sexual experience is not, however, dropped altogether. It reappears metaphorically, if not euphemistically, in the more desperate second act. When Winnie tells her autobiographical story about young Mildred (a name which in earlier versions was used for Winnie), Beckett includes an image of a mouse running up her leg, a sexual image. John Fletcher characterizes the narrative as a "burlesque tale of how little Mildred was deflowered by a mouse . . . ."[8]

The second excised scene dramatized Winnie's growing desperation, her overtly stated need for, if not communication itself, at least the illusion of communication, and the awareness of her isolation. The section follows an allusion to Cordelia's analysis of her estrangement from Lear, that not having "that glib and oily art . . . Hath lost me in your liking" (*Lear*, 1:1, 224, 233). The allusion suggests something of Winnie's exile.

> There was a time, do you remember, when once a month was enough for me . . . . Don't you remember? . . . Once a month! . . . Then once a fortnight . . . . The tally-sticks, don't you remember the tally-sticks, Edward, they must be lying about somewhere still, every thirtieth notch, then every fifteenth . . . . Then weekly, I would wake up as usual, refreshed for the day and without a care, for what is there to care about, and suddenly before I had time to as much as wash my teeth this feeling of anxiety—can he still hear me from his hole?—and I knew another week had flown . . . . Then finally daily . . . . One just wakes up and finds out . . . . This irritates you I know Edward, the first thing every morning, but it simplifies life for you in a way too at the same time, no more scorekeeping, that is what you should bear in mind when you refuse to satisfy me. (TS.-1, p. 8)

This incident is interesting for a number of reasons. First, Winnie has a reasonably accurate measure of the passage of time and is acutely aware of her growing desperation. The tally-sticks, as did the alarm clock, give her a means of measuring the passing of time. Neither her awareness nor her ability to measure time is conducive to the final comic tone of the first act, the dramatic irony which results from Winnie's inability to assess her condition accurately and the irony of hoping for change in a "heavenly" world where nothing changes. In the final version, Winnie approaches realization of her plight in Act II and then with less coherence as her thoughts become increasingly fragmented.

Second, the excised scene provides some concrete explanation of Winnie's opening, paradoxical behavior: she praises Willie's serenity and ability to sleep, yet wakes him violently. Willie has not responded to the alarm clock (and later the bell), and Winnie's motive for waking him is obscure at first. This excised section provides a rational explanation for her action and states a familiar Beckett theme explicitly: one reason for communication is to reassert one's own existence. Communication is thus a selfish act.

Winnie needs the security of knowing someone is there, listening, caring, testifying to her existence. As Beckett states in the preliminary remarks to *Film*, "*Esse est percipi.*"⁹ In the first typescript Winnie's need for the other, at least the illusion of another, is dramatically emphasized when Winnie, imitating Willie's voice, creates the illusion of a listener. Quoting Isaac Watt's version of Psalm 90, Winnie begins: "A thousand ages in thy sight are as an evening gone. (*Pause.*) Did you hear that, Edward? (*Pause. Imitating his voice.*) Yes. (*Own voice.*) What? (*Pause. Imitating his voice.*) A thousand ages in thy sight are as an evening gone" (TS.-1, p. 9). The fabricated exchange was no doubt an unnecessary restatement of Winnie's need, following closely, as it does, the actual exchange of the *Cymbeline* quotation, "Fear no more the heat o' the sun." The exchange also reveals that Winnie understands her needs more than Beckett would perhaps like. The section was cut and with it is lost a concrete example of how Winnie would readjust to a significant disturbance in her world, Willie's absence.

Third, the passage also conveys heavy sexual overtones: "do you remeber, when once a month was enough for me," and "that is what you should bear in mind when you refuse to satisfy me." Both statements may have seemed inappropriate to Winnie's final prudish characterization where she is revolted at the sight of Willie's pornographic postcard (although she examines it thoroughly) and is a little uncomfortable about having laughed at what she thought was Willie's reference to fornication. The casual sexual attitude of both the early Johnston and tally-stick episodes may have been particularly inappropriate to Winnie's traumatic response to retelling the autobiographical story of Mildred's rape. Although these last two major excisions brought the play closer to the final tone and thematic emphases, they have also decreased the development of Winnie's character and her condition, information which in a naturalistic play, for instance, would be the epiphany toward which the dramatist works.

The pattern of dramatic composition and revision described here reveals a struggle with development congruous with Beckett's distrust of language and realistic detail. As such, the method of composition of *Happy Days* appears consistent with the significant excisions Ruby Cohn describes in the *Endgame* manuscripts and Richard Admussen observed in the manuscripts of *Play*.¹⁰ While the earlier one-act version of *Happy Days* is not dramatically better than the final version (quite the contrary), it is in places more concrete and reveals more clearly the sort of images with which Beckett began, then grew away from, not toward a naturalistic, precisely-defined physical world, but toward an abstract clarity, an image free of cluttering detail. As Beckett has noted, "The difference between Joyce and myself is that Joyce was a synthesizer. He tried to pack the whole world into a book, in as much detail as possible, and I am an analyzer. I try to take as much of the detail away as possible."¹¹

Beckett's thematic commitment is to fundamental questions of reality, being and knowing, and not with their social manifestations. The composition of *Happy Days* reveals Beckett's own "contempt for the literature that 'describes,' for the realists and naturalists worshipping the offal of experience, prostrate before the epidermis and the swift epilepsy, and content to describe the surface, the facade, behind which the Idea is prisoner" (*Proust*, p. 59). The distaste for realistic detail is also present in Beckett's production *Regiebuch*. Beckett's description of the props reveals a desire to make them incongruous and unreal. The toothbrush, parasol, magnifying glass, and nail file all have disproportionately long handles. The revolver has a "disproportion between short butt & long muzzle" (*Regiebuch*, p. 81). The props are certainly incongruously funny, but the incongruity lifts them out of our familiar world. The revisions of *Happy Days* remind one of Beckett's attack on the painter, Tal Coat, who, he says, remains on the "plane of the feasible."[12] Beckett's own revisions demonstrate his "vaguening" the play, transcending the "plane of the feasible" to the unencumbered and abstracted view of man's irrationality, a view as unencumbered with social details as the mathematical symbol of irrationality, $\sqrt{2}$.

References

1. Beckett cited by Tom F. Driver, "Beckett by the Madeleine," *Columbia University Forum,* 4, No. 3 (1961), 23.

2. Colin Duckworth, "The Making of *Godot,*" *Casebook on 'Waiting for Godot,'* ed. Ruby Cohn, (New York: Grove Press, Inc., 1967), p. 94.

3. Richard L. Admussen, "The Manuscripts of Beckett's *Play,*" *Modern Drama,* 16 (June 1973), 24.

4. *Samuel Beckett: an exhibition,* ed. James Knowlson (London: Turret Books, 1971), p. 86.

5. Jan Kott, *Shakespeare Our Contemporary,* trans. Boleslaw Taborski, Anchor Books (Garden City, New York: Doubleday and Co., Inc, 1964), p. 133.

6. Samuel Beckett and Georges Duthuit, "Three Dialogues," *Samuel Beckett: A Collection of Critical Essays,* ed. Martin Esslin, Twentieth Century Views (Englewood Cliffs, N.J.: Prentice-Hall, 1965), p. 21.

7. Beckett cited by Driver, p. 22.

8. John Fletcher and John Spurling, *Beckett: A Study of His Plays* (New York: Hill and Wang, 1972), p. 102.

9. Samuel Beckett, *Film* (New York: Grove Press, Inc., 1969), p. 11

10. Admussen, pp. 23-27.

11. Beckett cited by Martin Esslin, "Beckett Symposium," *New Theatre Magazine,* 11, No. 3, p. 12.

12. "Three Dialogues," p. 17.

V

Low Comedy and the Antidote to Pathos

Happy Days has all the potential for pathetic dreariness. Its components presage melodrama—innocent female imprisoned, victim of injustice, attempts at freedom abandoned. A sentimental novelist might have written 900 pages on the heroine's exploits and her refusal to abandon hope. But *Happy Days* never degenerates into the exploitation of sentiment despite its sentimental heroine. The play was written by a comedian, one suckled on the Swiftian view of man and weaned on the travesties of two world wars and Irish politics. Beckett is a comedian, we must occasionally remind ourselves, funny as well as somber. He is at once clown, satirist, farceur, and nihilistic humorist like Lear's fool. The tradition on which his drama is nurtured is popular, vulgar, and comic, the underbelly of art: the circus, burlesque, vaudeville, music-hall, and silent film. Its staple is low comedy: slapstick routines, vulgar gestures, pratfalls, figures of speech literalized. "A man came up to me on the street and told me he hadn't had a bite all day, so I bit him." Beckett's theater is not quite the anti-art of Dada, but the comi-tragedy of Chaplin, Keaton, Laurel and Hardy, and the Marx Brothers. An early title Beckett contemplated for *Happy Days* was "A Low Comedy" (*ETE 56*, p. 40).

Beckett, however, like the dramatist to whom he is most often compared, Ionesco, claims to dislike the theater. "*I'm not interested in the theatre.* I very rarely go to see other people's plays."[1] But Beckett was attracted to the theater long before *Godot*. He acted in a number of student plays in Dublin[2] and one of his earliest artistic attempts was the satiric play, *Le Kid* 1931. And curiously, his characters are often conspicuously acting, putting on a play and creating effects on a gathering of people. In the major plays, *Godot, Endgame,* and *Happy Days*, the characters' consciousness of playing before an audience emerges as an important dramatic device. At one point, Vladimir refers to the audience as "that bog." Looking directly out toward the audience, Vladimir announces, "Not a soul in sight" (a remark perhaps prompted by the sparse houses Beckett observed at the small Paris theaters struggling to survive, or foresaw for the production of *Godot*). Hamm, like Pozzo, is a ham actor, euphuistic and histrionic. And one reason Hamm and Clov must go on, gray after gray, is that they are caught in a play, a tightly controlled game like existence itself. Clov asks, "What is there to keep me here?" Hamm's simple response, "The dialogue" (*Endgame*, p. 58). He even speaks of the agony of perpetuation in theatrical terms. As Hamm is warming up for his last soliloquy, Clov spies a young boy outside. Hamm: "More complications! . . . Not an underplot I trust" (*Endgame*, p. 78). And Winnie, going blind, has a fuzzy sense of being watched. In Act II of *Happy Days*, not only has Winnie returned to play her part for the audience, the audience has returned from the lobby to play its part for Winnie: "Someone is looking at me still. . . . Caring for me still. . . . That is what I find so wonderful. . . . Eyes on my eyes" (49-50). Those are our eyes![3]

The turn (or return) to playwrighting seems to have been a fortunate relief for Beckett. It forced a bifurcation of the single consciousness of the French fiction which was virtually at a cul-de-sac (though since had pushed on through the mud and fallen into a cylinder). The stage, of course, demands duality for conflict and dialogue, and repetitive public performance itself provides a visual metaphor for Beckett's cyclical view of existence. Dramatic performance is itself a symbol of almost identical recurrence. Night after night, the same events occur on stage. The same absurd agonies are inflicted on the same characters; they never seem to learn. Oedipus will return again tomorrow, sight restored, and blunder through the same dramatic ironies, exhibit the same hubris. Winnie-Willie, Clov-Hamm, Didi-Gogo will reappear tomorrow as they did today, as they did yesterday. Waiting. Again. And the characters' consciousness of their medium is itself a carefully calculated anti-realistic device, an attack on the artificial theater of illusion, on the suspension of disbelief. The improbabilities of trees sprouting leaves overnight, of night falling as abruptly as a guillotine blade, of consumed parasols reappearing are not only incongruously comic, but Beckett's means of freeing himself from theatrical realism and its concomitant obligation to explain and make plausible. As Beckett has argued, "art has nothing to do with clarity, does not dabble in the clear and does not make clear. . . ."[4] The unnatural events of the plays stand in defiance of the naturalistic tradition, but in sympathy with the unhinged world of the Marx Brothers.

Beckett's denial of interest in the theater is probably directed at the legitimate theater; Beckett's preference seems to be for the bastard. His plays testify to the author's thorough familiarity with the techniques of the dramatic substratum. They are nearly composites of fragments from popular entertainments, including especially the overt theatricality of vaudeville and the music-hall.

A story line swollen with sentimental potential and a sprinkling of dance-hall theatricality, of such stuff is *Happy Days* made. The balance of the two, of comedy and pathos, then, is of utmost importance. Comedy is Beckett's necessary counterweight to suffering, and Beckett's picture of man existing derives from that balance. At least part of the structural problem with *Fin de Partie* was the difficulty of balancing the tone of the play. Beckett struggled to shape the play to his preconceived structural plan. In a note preceding the first typescript of *Fin de Partie*, Beckett writes, "Act 1. *Hilare,* Act 2. *Mortellement triste.*"[5] But the play would not conform; it insisted on its own shape. The two-act version reveals very little tonal difference between the two acts, and consequently Beckett abandoned the two-act structure. Shaping the relationship of comedy and pathos to produce the play's final tone is a structural problem as crucial as shaping the pattern of dramatic action or the number of acts a play will have. Shaping *Krapp's Last Tape*, for instance, Beckett added much of the comic material after the central situation of the play was formed. As Professor Knowlson notes of the "Krapp" section of the *ETE 56* notebook, "There is no mention at all at this stage of the by-play with the bananas that was to open the printed text. . . . On the other hand, most of the incidents that are referred to by Krapp and his reflections upon them are already present in this first draft." Much of the comic counterweight is added in the second typescript: "The second typescript sheet includes the lengthy description of Krapp's actions with bananas and keys which figures in the printed text."[6] In the *Happy Days* manuscripts the pattern of composition, of tonal adjustment is similar. Throughout the composition of *Happy Days*, Beckett carefully manipulates the balance of comedy and pathos, and most of the comic counterweight is added after the play's central action is set. The following discussion traces the play's developing tone as Beckett adjusts and manipulates the physical comedy of the play.

Beckett's initial problem was to balance the tone of the opening scene. His first impulse was to make the opening tableau more obviously comic than it is in its final form, an attempt no doubt to counter the austerity of the setting and the seriousness of Winnie's entombment. In the first draft (*ETE 56*) Willie appears at the rise of the curtain asleep and dressed like a circus clown. Beckett describes him as follows: "*his back to the audience, a man, in striped pyjamas.* [He is?] *sleeping, hanging so far forward that only his buttocks and foreshortened back are visible, his arms on his knees and his head on his arms. Bare flesh between trousers and coat of pyjamas*" (*ETE 56*, pp. 36-37). In the first full holograph version (H-1), Beckett added that the stripes of Willie's pyjamas match those on Winnie's parasol. The tableau, Winnie buried up to above her waist and beside her the buttocks and legs of Willie, was to be held for 30 seconds (an assault on the audience's patience and shortened in revision to the final "*Long pause*"). Presenting the audience with half of each character, Beckett would certainly have reinforced visually a familiar theme, a world where "Nothing is ontologically whole . . . objects and persons are predetermined to be partial. . . ."[7] The tableau would also have dramatized the complementary nature of the two characters, a pattern of Cartesian characterization of which Beckett is fond in the drama (e.g., Lucky-Pozzo, Gogo-Didi, Clov-Hamm), but the visual joke, virtually an indecent exposure, would have drawn attention away from Winnie and her opening monologue; and evidently Beckett felt her opening speech was crucial. The dominant pattern of most of the play is not the relationship between Willie and Winnie (for the play is almost a total monologue and designed as such from its early stages), but the disjunction between Winnie's plight and her attitude (her understanding, or its lack), a disjunction reinforced by the physical contrast between the starkness of the set and Winnie's physical vanity. In the third stage (TS.-1) Willie (then Bee) is eliminated from the opening, hidden from view, and the audience's attention remains limited to the incongruities surrounding Winnie's inexplicable burial. With the removal of the potentially distracting scene featuring Willie's semi-exposed buttocks, Winnie's ironic praise of the changelessness of heaven is finally placed between our initial shock at Winnie and the beginning of her morning ritual (having brushed her teeth, she spits out the residue). The final effect remains comic, serious predicament undercut with vulgar gesture, without being burlesque, a pattern close to some of the revisions Beckett made in the *Fin de Partie* manuscripts. In an early version Hamm at one point decided, perhaps like Noah repopulating the world after the flood, that he needed to engender a large family. Clov appears in disguise "wearing a blond wig, false breasts, and a skirt over his trousers."[8] In the final versions of both plays, ostentatious dress is reserved for the end, when character focus shifts. In *Endgame* attention shifts from Hamm to Clov at the end as Clov prepares to leave. He enters outlandishly dressed. In *Happy Days*, Willie becomes the focus of the play as he enters, "dressed to kill."

The scene with Willie dressed in ill-fitting pyjamas was never restored to the play, and consequently Beckett was left with the problem of introducing him. With his original appearance cut, he made his entrance when Winnie woke him with her ominous-looking parasol. He was then a direct victim of Winnie's careless cruelty. Unlike his earlier introduction as a sleepy clown, his appearance with a physical injury would certainly not be burlesque, but it also had the potential to force an unwanted shift in focus. Had he been in pain or agony after the beating, had he complained about the injury, the scene might have degenerated into early pathos, but the injury is ignored. (Ten years later, however, Beckett changed his mind. Directing the German production, Beckett had Willie respond with three cries: two when he is struck by Winnie's parasol, the third when hit with the medicine bottle.)[9] In the first holograph, Beckett entertained the possibility that Winnie might understand the damage she had done to Willie's skull: "Poor Tom I have opened your [skull?]" (H-1,

p. 9). But the realization was immediately cut. As the scene stood in the first holograph, Winnie bangs Willie over the head with her weapon, the bloody head pops up—propinquity of events suggests cause and effect. But Beckett, troubled by the incident from the first, wrote it out three times in the first holograph without substantive change. Apparently he intended to change the scene twice, but the same words returned. The following is the version Beckett let stand in the first holograph: "*She strikes down with beak of parasol. Pause. She strikes again, the back of a bald head, trickling blood, rises into view above slope. Pause. She strikes again*" (H-1, p. 10). The overkill of the third blow, after Willie's head was visible, helped create the impression that Winnie was unaware of the effects of her action, a characteristic lack of awareness. But the scene as originally presented contained two major problems in addition to the potential shift in focus: first, it revealed a cruel streak in Winnie early in the play, and second, Willie was the direct victim of Winnie's cruelty, a cruelty for which we can see a rational, albeit accidental, cause. As noted in Chapter IV, however, Beckett is revising away from such precisely defined conflict. Professor Cohn notes a similar problem with tone in the *Endgame* revisions. As some of the comic scenes were eliminated, so were the cruelest scenes.[10] In one, for instance, on the day of Nell's death, Hamm orders Clov to put Nagg's head in a pillory to prevent his withdrawing into the ash can. In the *Happy Days* revisions, Winnie still strikes down at Willie with her parasol, but we are never certain that the blows bloody his head; the early suggestion of direct cruelty is eliminated. Beckett did not, however, want to scrap the image of Willie's bloody head altogether. The difficulty was solved by having Willie's head appear after Winnie haphazardly discards her medicine bottle, "*in WILLIE'S direction.*"

To weaken Winnie's culpability further and keep the conflict moving toward the vague, Willie does not appear immediately after the crash. His appearance is delayed momentarily until Winnie is preoccupied with trying to remember a literary quotation. The incident then fulfills the additional purpose of undercutting Winnie's contemplation. When Willie finally appears, Beckett adds comic touches: Willie spreads his handkerchief on his head, then puts on his boater, complete with club ribbon, over the handkerchief. The actions could belong to a vaudeville song and dance man. These two revisions are completed by the first typescript (TS.-1) with the result that the first time we see much of Willie is after the bottle-throwing episode. His hand appears earlier to return the parasol which slipped from Winnie's hand (a fine chivalrous touch), but we do not see the bulk of him until Winnie smashes the medicine bottle over his head.

The revisions of Willie's initial appearance demonstrate Beckett's ability to solve a multitude of problems with a minimum of alteration. Willie is still comic without being a distraction; Winnie has still created some havoc, but the suggestion of malice in her nature has been removed; and as Willie becomes the victim of Winnie's haphazard toss of the bottle, both he and she appear to be victims of some ill-defined cosmic plot, a direction crucial to the vaguening of the play. We are, finally, never really certain how Willie's head was injured. Winnie may have hit him with the parasol or with the medicine bottle, or as a curious variation on the Cartesian split, Winnie's action may have had nothing to do with Willie's injured head. The only relationship between Winnie's action and Willie's appearance may be a temporal propinquity, the connection our own *post hoc, ergo propter hoc* fallacy. These changes are characteristic of the shaping and tightening of material in the early version, and through them not only do we see Beckett's balancing of comic and pathetic incidents, we have a glimpse of his dramatic art, his ability to shape and compress his material.

The medicine bottle figures prominently in another set of early revisions in *Happy Days*, as an example of Beckett's manipulation of comic technique and his tendency to move toward physical comedy in the drama, a pattern, incidentally, in contrast to that which Professor Cohn observes in *Endgame*, where "the center of non-gravity shifts from the visual to the verbal."[11] Early in the play Winnie seeks some relief from a bottle of medicine (as if somehow medicine for the body can relieve the angst of modern existence). In the earliest versions much of the humor is verbally reminiscent of some of Joyce's tonguetwisters, as Winnie reads the poetic and solecistic directions on the bottle: "Two double dessert spoonfuls five or six times daily before and . . . (*bends closer, moistens fingers, rubs label, reads*) . . . after food" (H-1, p. 12). As the scene is revised, the joke gradually becomes more visual and the irony increases. The earliest revision, on the verso of the first holograph, heightens the irony by adding the hyperbolic promise of relief: "Relief . . . (*bends closer*) . . . instantaneous" (H-1, p. 11). The possibility of relief is then sharply undercut as the amount of medicine in the bottle decreases from "partly empty" to "¾ empty" in the first draft, to the "almost empty" of the final version; even if the medicine did work, adequate dosage is unavailable. By the final version, the linguistic banter is played down: the hope is heightened by specifically enumerating the ailments the potion might cure: "Loss of spirits . . . lack of keenness . . . want of appetite . . . infants . . . children . . . adults . . . six level tablespoonfuls daily . . . before and after meals." The undercutting is accomplished with physical action: "(*Takes off spectacles, lays them down, holds up bottle at arm's length to see level . . .*)" (13). Hopefully, if the eyes of the audience are not as bad as Winnie's, they can see that she is holding an "*almost empty bottle of red medicine . . . .*" This type of change demonstrates not only Beckett's movement away from linguistic humor, but also his craftsmanship—he turns a relatively minor irony into a major one as hope is introduced only to be instantly shattered. The physical joke reinforces Winnie's hopeful nature as well as the impossibility of the relief Winnie seeks throughout the play.

Beckett's shaping of the scene in which Winnie discovers the emmet is another example of his exploiting a scene's comic possibilities. After Winnie discovers the emmet carrying eggs, a sign that despite the hellish environment life will go on, and Willie makes his one and only sensory observation, that the mention of the ant makes him feel as though insects were crawling over his skin, Winnie mistakes the comment, "Formication," for a sexual reference (as no doubt most of the audience does). This is the one part of the play when the two seem to enjoy themselves (a temporary union in the pineal gland); ironically, the enjoyment stems from misunderstanding. The earliest versions do not exploit the full comic possibilities of the scene: "*Edward laughs quietly. After a moment she joins in. They laugh quietly together. Edward stops laughing. She laughs on alone. She stops laughing*" (H-1, p. 40). In the final version Beckett develops the scene's comic potential: "(*Pause. WILLIE laughs quietly. After a moment she joins in. They laugh quietly together. WILLIE stops. She laughs on a moment alone. WILLIE joins in. They laugh together. She stops. WILLIE laughs on a moment alone*)" (30). In addition to exploiting the slapstick potential of the scene, the revision creates a more symmetrically balanced episode, ending where it began, Willie laughing solo. And finally, the scene helps to undercut the following partial realization by Winnie: "Or were we perhaps diverted by two quite different things?" (31). As Ruby Cohn notes, "In turning to the theater . . . Beckett uses action to help him undermine language."[12]

The revisions of the medicine bottle routine and the emmet misunderstanding are vivid examples of Beckett's development of comic action as a tonic, an elixir against the infection of pathos. For Beckett's plays are susceptible. His characters are in desperate circumstances, victims whose failures are outside the self; they have been programmed to fail. We must cry or laugh, and laughter is at once more therapeutic and more bitter, for we are laughing at disaster. Beckett himself has described Willie's laugh as *rire jaune*, a bitter laugh.[13] Comic physical action is used throughout the play's first act to undermine and subvert the impact of the desperation of Winnie's plight. In addition, pathos is attacked surgically, by excising material which builds sympathy for Winnie. The tally-stick episode and the sexual assault of the early Johnston-Cooker episode discussed in Chapter IV were scenes which increased audience sympathy for Winnie and created a fuller human being, one who, at least to some extent, was aware of her own desperate plight. But sympathy and full characterization are anti-comic. By eliminating and undercutting highly emotional scenes, or scenes which help develop Winnie's character and audience sympathy for her, Beckett allows the irony, incongruity, parody, and paradox of the early scenes to dominate.

Another scene in which Beckett's revisions help shift the tonal pattern of the play toward the comic includes one of the few extended bits of dialogue between the two characters, the repetition of the *Cymbeline* quotation. The exchange further dramatizes Winnie's need to have someone testify to her existence. The earlier versions of the scene tend to be more sentimental than the later, and differ from the final in two significant ways, both of which would have engaged our sympathies and plunged us into the emotion of the encounter. In the earliest versions, Winnie's voice actually falters during the episode, her physical deterioration obvious at this point in the play. Her voice grows softer and softer to the final *"very soft."* In a verso note, Beckett entertained the possibility that Winnie recognizes her growing desperation: "even were it [the voice] to fail as just now for [some reason?] or other to little more than a murmur . . ." (H-1, p. 31). Second, Willie followed her faltering and one could sense some affection in his reduction of voice to follow hers. The episode contained a tenderness as it was presented in the first holograph and typescript. We almost realize that once, in the old days when things were done in the "old style," love existed. And out of Winnie's selfish need to have someone testify to her existence, bred "a relationship which might—almost—give a reality to friendship and make something other than a clownish farce of love."[14]

But that is emotion, and emotion is the staple of melodrama and tragedy, not nihilistic *humor noir*. In revision, tenderness is excised, Winnie's faltering voice and Willie's understanding expunged, replaced with hostility. Willie's responses to Winnie's requests for repetition are violent, irritated, and finally, *"more irritated."*

But Beckett's most frequently wielded weapon against pathos is the comic gesture, the illiberal jest. To Winnie's pompous moral indignation over Willie's pornographic postcard Beckett adds, *"takes nose between left forefinger and thumb"* (19). And the precision of the directions suggests a stylized action which would increase the comic. Shortly thereafter, Winnie is threatened by involuntary memory and forced to look within. "What *is* the alternative? . . . What *is* the al-" (20). Beckett decimates the seriousness of Winnie's plight by adding, *"WILLIE blows nose loud and long . . . ."* Willie then spreads his handkerchief on his head to dry, with, no doubt, stylized mannerisms. Both comic incidents were added late in the play's composition, TS.-3 and H-3 respectively, after the two-act structure was established.

Many of the comic activities Beckett includes in his drama reflect the theatrical tradition in which he works, music-hall and vaudeville, those modern vestiges of low comedy and improvisation epitomized in the *Commedia dell'Arte* in which stock characters improvised around a set routine, the *lazzo*. Beckett's drama is not, of course, improvised, quite the contrary, but it makes extensive use of the *lazzo*.

The *lazzo* finds its way into modern drama chiefly through the early comic film. *Duck Soup*, the 1933 Marx Brothers classic, for example, incorporates a number of such set pieces brought over from vaudeville. Pinkie (Harpo) finds what he believes to be the combination to Mrs. Teasedale's (Margaret Dumont) safe. He tries the combination on what looks like a safe. Loud brass band blares from the radio. Pinkie turns the dial to silence it; it comes off in his hand. He tries to muffle the sound with a cushion, then with a curtain. He sprays it with seltzer, throws it inside the closet; it shatters, but keeps playing. He retrieves it and smashes it to bits with a huge ashtray. Music continues. Only after the pieces are thrown out the window and the window closed, does the music cease. In *Happy Days*, Beckett's persistent parasol, mirror, and the day itself are variations on Harpo's indestructible radio. Of Beckett's theater, Michael Robinson notes:

> Beckett's sympathy with the pure, non-literary theatre is evident in the particular and the general structure of his plays. Lucky's famous speech with its confusion of garbled knowledge recalls the Doctor in ancient farce while the improvisation of the two tramps suggests the endless semantic speculations and misunderstandings of the *Commedia dell'Arte* .... In the plays the ceaseless linguistic permutations of the novels are replaced by equally pedantic and mechanical physical permutations. If language does threaten to assert itself, its pretensions are burst by the pratfall.[15]

The exchange of bowlers in *Godot*, Clov's antics with step ladder and telescope, Krapp's slipping on his banana peel, the cat and dog routine in *Film*, are all stock routines. In *Happy Days* Beckett relies on the arrested or suspended gesture, where a character is interrupted in mid-action and holds an awkward position for a brief tableau. Beckett uses the technique three separate times in *Happy Days*. All three instances appear in the first draft and during potentially emotional scenes: 1. Winnie tries to don her hat as Willie reads from the newspaper; each time she begins, Willie's reading interrupts her; 2. immediately after the hat routine, the *lazzo* is reversed; Winnie interrupts Willie's fanning as she reads from the toothbrush handle; and finally, 3. after spotting the emmet, Winnie tries to put down her glasses and is interrupted by Willie's comments, first about the eggs, then about formication. The last two routines remain unchanged in the play's seven versions, but the first undergoes significant alteration. In the first sequence of suspended gestures, Willie is reading about a variety of aberrant rockets striking various cities (see Chapter IV). The awkwardness of Winnie's action serves to undercut the seriousness of what was probably a nuclear world war. When reference to the holocaust was cut in the second holograph, the suspended gesture was retained and distributed through Winnie's two reminiscences, the first about Charley Hunter, the second about Mr. Johnston. The purpose of the *lazzo*, however, remains; the suspended gesture serves as a counterpoint to her reminiscences, further undercutting their seriousness.

What is obvious about the bulk of Beckett's revisions of *Happy Days* is that he consciously worked to develop the comic and undercut the pathetic, but the major revisions are made in Act I. Act II is another matter. The clown has been injured; he struggles through his routine, but it is no longer funny. His pain is obvious. Winnie's plight is intensified by the absence of Willie and the further restriction on her habits, her protection. Yet, pathetically, she clings to her hope. Her ritual is altered, but not because of a loss of faith. She may omit prayer, for instance, not because she has lost faith in a benign supreme being, but because she can no longer fold her hands, an integral part of her ritual. She struggles to salvage what portions of her habit she can; she distends her cheeks, pouts, but in her determination she grows pathetic, as the audience is painfully aware of her desperation. Her physical action is limited and she is forced to rely more on words, especially her autobiography.

Willie is absent, Winnie's physical mobility severely restricted. The comic possibilities decrease since much of the earlier comedy relied on the interplay of two characters and physical action. In Act II, Winnie restates her memories and fears, but they are fragmented, virtually incoherent as the disintegration of her personality is reflected syntactically. We are confronted with her physical deterioration. Additional memories intrude. An idyllic day on the lake, reminiscent of Krapp's sexual encounter. But her praise of the day continues, and as it does the ironies intensify. The pathetic potential of Act I, carefully restrained by the manipulation of physical comedy, is released in the second act. The ironies remain, but now they intensify the pathetic. As Ruby Cohn observes, "Irony serves, finally, to intensify the pathetic as well as the comic."[16]

Beckett's exact thinking in structuring the play's final tone is difficult to assess. Many of the comic revisions occur in the first typescript and the second holograph, the point evidently when Beckett was deciding on a second act. But we are finally caught in the chicken-egg cycle. Was the decision to include a second act necessitated by the decision to cut some of the concrete characterization of Winnie, or did the decision to write a second act force the excisions and the development of the comedy of the first? Beckett's manuscript revisions will not answer the question. But one point is obvious: the major tonal alterations of *Happy Days* occur at a point when the play begins moving toward the two-act structure. And at that point, Beckett labored to keep the focus of the play on Winnie and develop the comic potential of Act I by exploiting the techniques of popular entertainments. The result is a tonal pattern close to the one Beckett had planned for the two-act *Fin de Partie:* "Act 1. *Hilare,* Act 2. *Mortellement triste.*"

References

1. Colin Duckworth, *Angels of Darkness* (New York: Barnes & Noble Books, 1972), p. 17.

2. John Fletcher, *Samuel Beckett's Art* (New York: Barnes & Noble, Inc., 1967), p. 43.

3. cf. Ruby Cohn, "Plays and Players in the Plays of Samuel Beckett," *Yale French Studies*, 29 (Spring-Summer 1962), 43-48.

4. Samuel Beckett, "Denis Devlin," *Transition: Tenth Anniversary*, 27 (April-May 1938), 289-294.

5. Manuscript on deposit at The Ohio State University Library.

6. *Samuel Beckett: an exhibition*, catalogue by James Knowlson (London: Turret Books, 1971), p. 80.

7. Ihab Hassan, *The Literature of Silence* (New York: Alfred A. Knopf, Inc., 1967), p. 132.

8. Ruby Cohn, "The Beginning of *Endgame*," *Modern Drama*, 9 (December 1966), 321.

9. Ruby Cohn, "Beckett Directs *Happy Days*," *Performance*, 1, No. 2 (April 1972), 117.

10. Ruby Cohn, "The Beginning of *Endgame*," p. 322.

11. *Ibid.*, p. 323.

12. Ruby Cohn, *Samuel Beckett: The Comic Gamut* (New Brunswick, N.J.: Rutgers University Press, 1962), p. 208.

13. Ruby Cohn, "Beckett Directs *Happy Days*," p. 116.

14. Richard N. Coe, *Samuel Beckett* (New York: Grove Press, Inc., 1968), p. 82.

15. Michael Robinson, *The Long Sonata of the Dead: A Study of Samuel Beckett* (New York: Grove Press, Inc., 1969), p. 237.

16. Ruby Cohn, *Samuel Beckett: The Comic Gamut*, p. 136.

VI

A New Mythological Reality: The Literary Allusions in *Happy Days*

Discussing *Godot* with Beckett, Colin Duckworth asked, "Is a Christian interpretation of the play justified?" Beckett responded, "Yes, Christianity is a mythology with which I am perfectly familiar. So naturally I use it."[1] The response is something of an understatement, for Beckett's corpus is saturated with Christian mythology and variations on its ideology. He is as tied to Christian thought as Lucky is to Pozzo, as obsessed with Christian dogma and its implications as was Joyce. Maria Jolas suggests, "Like Joyce he is also a Christ-haunted man . . . ."[2] And little wonder. Born 13 April 1906. Friday the thirteenth. Good Friday the thirteenth. On the 606th anniversary of Dante's descent into Hell. A persistent theme of Beckett's is divine caprice, the arbitrary nature of salvation, a theme which haunts his plays like the ghost of King Hamlet. In *Godot,* one of Estragon's feet is comfortable, one in pain; one of his feet is saved, one damned. Beckett is fond of quoting a sentence from Augustine (ostensibly for its shape): "Do not despair; one of the thieves was saved. Do not presume; one of the thieves was damned."[3] The sentence indeed has a fine shape and balance, but it imposes shape on chaos. The symmetry of the sentence veils the horror of arbitrary salvation, a frequent torment for Beckett's characters. What are the reasons that one thief was saved, one damned? What had they done or said? Why is the story treated in only one of the four gospels? What is the reason for God's refusal of Cain's gift, his acceptance of Abel's? Was Cain somehow forewarned that God expected his chosen to remain nomadic shepherds and not farm the land? Had He something against sod-busters? The questions suggest the failure of a covenant of benevolence, the failure of love and order. Beckett's characters are hounded by the inconsistencies of a system, of systems, which have dominated the western world at least since Christ. Moran, and hence the Unnamable, may be speaking directly for Beckett as he ponders: "Certain questions of a theological nature preoccupied me strangely" (*Three Novels*, p. 166).

Beckett is, of course, preoccupied with mythologies other than Christian, and their promise, their pretense to order haunts him as well. His works exude the mythos and ethos of western civilization. In his first important essay, "Dante . . . Bruno . Vico . . Joyce," a defense of Joyce's *Work in Progress*, Beckett placed Joyce in a developing western, intellectual tradition by comparing him to the three Italian writers. Beckett's characters often appear to exist in isolation, but they play their roles against a backdrop made from the shattered traditions of western man. In *Molloy*, for instance, Beckett continues the variegated development of the epic form, most recently manipulated by Joyce. *Molloy*, however, is still another development, a contrapuntal epic, played fugally—two epic journeys. It is also a parody of the novel itself, a middle-class form which developed with Richardson and Defoe, and which, under the guise of verisimilitude, has carried on an orgy with things, objects, portable possessions, the stuff of middle-class lives. As Hugh Kenner observes, somewhat hyperbolically, "The trilogy is, among other things, a compendious abstract of all the novels that have ever been written, reduced to their most general terms."[4] And philosophical systems are not spared. Beckett's *oeuvre* echoes and re-echoes western philosophical traditions from Zeno and Pythagoras to Wittgenstein and Sartre. His characters are invariably either committed to systems which fail, which must fail, or haunted by the failure of systems. They are fascinated and befuddled by the problems of Eleatic paradoxes, the Pythagorean incommensurability of side and diagonal, Cartesian bifurcation, Phenomenology, Logical Positivism, and Existentialism.[5] In response, indeed almost in defense, Beckett's literary critics have often been forced (at times unfortunately) to deal more with philosophy than art in their groping to understand.

The tradition within which Beckett works, however, includes not only western man's literary forms and philosophical systems, but popular culture as well. The title itself was chosen to reflect a cheery toast and the popular song, "Happy Days are Here Again."

The mythological reality with which Beckett works is then a complicated pastiche, a patch quilt worth careful scrutiny. The mythic peregrinations of Odysseus provided Joyce with a framework for *Ulysses*. The single myth was for Joyce both skeleton and foil, and was used virtually allegorically. As Eliot saw in 1923, Joyce manipulated "a continuous parallel between contemporaneity and antiquity." The Odyssian myth was for Joyce a "way of controlling, of ordering, of giving shape."[6] In his most allegorical works, Beckett too wove his tale around a single myth, not so much to order and control as to universalize and ironize. Myth is never for Beckett a skeleton on which to hang his contemporary flesh. During the thirty-odd seconds of "Breath," Beckett has hardly time for one allusion: the Biblical version of creation: "And the Lord God formed man . . . and breathed into his nostrils the breath of life" (*Genesis,* 2:7). Naturally, twentieth-century philosophers were not the first to contemplate the paradoxical nature and absurdity of existence; neither were they the first to devise images of perpetual agony. Beckett draws freely on Greek and early Christian images of torment. From Dante, Beckett borrows the image of the indolent Belacqua. And without being direct allegories, "Act Without Words, I" calls to mind the frustrations of Tantalus, "Act Without Words, II," Sisyphus (divaricated). The myths are not a framework, but the mythic echoes help equate the daily frustrations of modern man with those torments devised by our fathers, the Greeks and early Christians, to punish the sinners, the defiant, the vain, and the slothful. In Beckett's vision, of course, the justice of punishment is removed, and everyman suffers. And the mythic echoes emphasize the repetitive nature of experience, for Beckett a convenient means of illustrating his cyclical view of history.

Beckett's use of a single myth is, however, rare. Even Joyce realized that too close an allegorical pattern may be restrictive ultimately. "I may have oversystematized *Ulysses,*"[7] he confessed. The Verticalist manifesto, "Poetry is Vertical," 1932 (and Verticalism is the one literary movement to which Beckett has allowed his name to be linked, albeit loosely), contains a rejection of Eliot's appeal for a return to classicism. The manifesto proclaims, "We are against the renewal of the classical ideal." But again, Beckett's ties with the Verticalists were slight, and as he himself had warned in 1929, "The danger is in the neatness of identifications." The manifesto, however, goes on to proclaim an interest in a new mythic reality, as opposed, evidently, to a classically mythic reality: "The synthesis of a true collectivism is made possible by a community of spirits who aim at the construction of a new mythological reality."[8] While Beckett has evidently not been much interested in "a community of spirits," his composition of *Happy Days* reveals a continuing interest in "a new mythological reality" formed from fragments of great western traditions shattered or decaying. The mythic reality is not an allegorical rendering. We see instead, the backdrop of western thought in jagged fragments, like a collage of found objects, the draff of Winnie's education. The fragmented mythic pattern parallels the way in which Beckett presents the background of his characters through their minced and quasi-objectified autobiographies. Each of Beckett's works, in a Miltonic echo, is a rendering of paradise lost, or more precisely, of paradise denied. And the pervasive myth is a composite, a montage of western culture, which, like the *Bible* specifically, is a hope unbloomed. It is painfully obvious, for instance, that the Lord does not uphold "all that fall." The particular literary allusions in *Happy Days* take on a mythic quality as they reverberate throughout the play as Eliot's Fisher King myth echoes through *The Waste Land*. Beckett's mythic pattern is not as classical and structural as Eliot's though. He provides no footnotes, no single key like Eliot's reference to Weston's *From Ritual to Romance*. The mythic pattern of *Happy Days* is closer to the way in which the spirit of America permeates Hart Crane's *The Bridge*. But Beckett's backdrop is vaster and more fragmented than Crane's, and without a central, single, unifying symbol.

Creation of the cultural montage is an integral part of the making, the shaping of *Happy Days*. The collection of literary allusions Winnie tries to recall is part of her old style, part of her attempt to maintain order. The tendency of Winnie to reach back into her school-days literature was part of Beckett's design as early as the first full holograph (H-1). As she realizes that her lipstick is running out, Beckett notes: "*Lips. First words of famous line–transitoriness of all things–Bible possibly . . .*" (TS.-1, p. 3). After the *Cymbeline* exchange, Winnie's sense of estrangement is reflected in her quoting Cordelia after her disinheritance (see Chapter III). The earliest use of allusion appears local, however, a parallel to Winnie's immediate condition. As the play grows, a more complicated pattern of allusion develops. Fragments of literary quotations are added throughout the play's composition, allusions in which themes and a pattern of imagery are surprisingly consistent. And literary references only obliquely suggested in early drafts are emphasized, clarified, and re-stated as the play develops. Throughout, Winnie recalls fragments of the old culture without fully understanding the ironies in the contrast with her present condition. And the growing number of allusions is not only part of Beckett's attempt to universalize Winnie's struggle, but an ironic commentary on a school girl's intellectual tradition—her references are not, afer all, as esoteric as Watt's or Murphy's. Winnie's allusions are interwoven with her other habits and add to her ability to go on. Allusions are used, notes Lawrence Harvey, "in a . . .closely integrated . . . fabric . . . in his later . . . writings—in *Happy Days,* for example." [9]

Most critics, however, have paid only passing attention to the pattern of literary allusions in *Happy Days,* often assuming that identifying the quotations is sufficient, an indication that the speaker is another avatar of Beckett's scholar-tramps. But even the identification has been incomplete and occasionally misleading. Professor Cohn's identification of the phrase the "old style" with Dante is a significant contribution to our understanding of the complexity of Beckett's literary allusions in *Happy Days:* "Winnie's 'old style' is implicitly contrasted with Dante's *dolce stil nuovo;* she even utters the phrase 'sweet old style.' Dante's *dolce stil nuovo* ushered in the vigorous literature of the Renaissance, but by the time of *Happy Days* that Renaissance has become a weary decadence." And she identifies most, but not all, of Winnie's quotations, arguing that they have a function in the immediate situation, to "emphasize the *un*happiness of the human condition," and a more general purpose: the "literary echoes" along with Winnie's other ritualized activities ("the inventory of possessions, the repetitive refrains, the constant doubts and denials") are part of her "attempts to fill the void of existence."[10] And so they are. Yet, they are more. The quotations do not all point to human woe. One quotation Professor Cohn fails to identify evokes a nineteenth-century, romantic, hedonistic ideal. Winnie's "paradise enow" is an allusion to Edward FitzGerald's translation of *The Rubáiyát of Omar Khayyám*. Another, "damask" cheek is a reference to Shakespeare's *Twelfth Night*, a comedy of mistaken identities firmly rooted in the *Commedia dell'Arte*. And certainly the duet from *The Merry Widow* reflects more joy than despair. Ihab Hassan complicates matters by suggesting that the play contains a reference to the *Song of Songs*,[11] but Hassan does not specify the allusion, and to date it has defied precise identification. We may guess that perhaps Hassan considers Winnie's song to be a parody of the wedding song, but such an association is tenuous and receives no support from the play.

The allusions, then, function on a broader level than additional aids to Winnie's adaptation or as a means of establishing a somber mood. They are also a crucial adjunct of the play's central irony. The snippets of quotations are designed to function most effectively when they call to mind the broader context of the work alluded to. As Winnie recites her classroom exercises to fill time and check her own physical deterioration, the cumulative weight of the quotations, as they reverberate and are orchestrated throughout the play, form Beckett's mythic pattern. As John Fletcher suggests (but unfortunately, never elaborates), Beckett's examination of man's contemporary predicament "is structured in the form of myth."[12] The examples of Beckett's use of Dante's *dolce stil nuovo*, the endlessness of Winnie's Eleatic burial, the addition of the fragment from the Lesser Doxology, "World without end, Amen," and the pervasiveness of images of fundamental changelessness under the sun and human vanity echoing *Ecclesiastes* (the last two discussed in Chapter III), demonstrate the ways in which fragments of Christian mythology and western intellectual tradition help provide the mythic structure of the play.

Fortunately for the critic who has access to the *Happy Days* manuscripts, Beckett has taken the trouble to note in the margin of the final typescript (TS.-4) the exact references to most of the specific literary fragments Winnie recalls. Clearly Beckett intended these references to be an integral part of the play, since in his pre-production correspondence with Alan Schneider he carefully prepared a list of Winnie's literary references for the director, a list which, incidentally, includes one more quotation than Beckett's notes in the fourth typescript (see Appendix B for a complete listing). He also suggested to Schneider that as Winnie's personality deteriorates, the quality of the literature to which she alludes also declines, a point which Professor Cohn echoes:

WINNIE (arresting gesture). What?
         Pause.
WILLIE   Formication.
         Pause. She lays down spectacles, gazes before her. Finally.
WINNIE   (murmur). God. (Pause. WILLIE laughs quietly. After a
         moment she joins in. They laugh quietly together. WILLIE
         stops. She laughs on a moment alone. WILLIE joins in.
         They laugh together. She stops. WILLIE laughs on a moment
         alone. He stops. Pause. Normal voice.) Ah well what a joy
         in any case to hear you laugh again, Willie, I was con-
         vinced I never would, you never would. (Pause.) I suppose
         some people might think us a trifle irreverent, but I
         doubt it. (Pause.) How can one better magnify the Almighty
         than by sniggering with him at his little jokes, particular-
         ly the poorer ones? (Pause.) I think you would back me up
         there, Willie. (Pause.) Or were we perhaps diverted by
         two quite different things? (Pause.) Oh well, what does
         it matter, that is what I always say, so long as one...
         you know...what is that wonderful line...laughing wild...
         something something laughing wild amid severest woe.
         (Pause.) And now? (Long pause.) Was I lovable once, Willie?
         (Pause.) Was I ever lovable? (Pause.) Do not misunderstand
         my question, I am not asking you if you loved me, we know
         all about that, I am asking you if you found me lovable -
         at one stage. (Pause.) No? (Pause.) You can't? (Pause.)
         Well I admit it is a teaser. And you have done more than
         your bit already, for the time being, just lie back now
         and relax, I shall not trouble you again unless I am com-
         pelled to, just to know you are there within hearing and
         conceivably on the semi-alert is...er...happiness enow.
         (Pause.) The day is now well advanced. (Smile.) To speak
         in the old style. (Smile off.) And yet it is perhaps a little
         soon for my song. (Pause.) To sing too soon is a great
         mistake, I find. (Turning towards bag.) There is of course
         the bag. (Looking at bag.) The bag. (Back front.) Could
         I enumerate its contents? (Pause.) No. (Pause.) Could I,
         if some kind person were to come along and ask, What all
         have you got in that big black bag, Winnie? give an ex-
         haustive answer? (Pause.) No. (Pause.) The depths in par-
         ticular, who knows what treasures. (Pause.) What comforts.
         (Turns to look at bag.) Yes, there is the bag. (Back
         front.) But something tells me, Do not overdo the bag,
         Winnie, make use of it of course, let it help you...along,
         when stuck, by all means, but cast your mind forward,
         something tells me, cast your mind forward, Winnie, to
         the time when words must fail - (she closes eyes, pause,
         opens eyes) - and do not overdo the bag. (Pause. She turns

In Act II, "She actually quotes from such sentimental versifiers as Charles Wolfe, rather than from the great poets of the English language."[13] The judgment is at least open to question, since in Act II Winnie also quotes from Milton, Keats, Shakespeare, and Yeats, as well as Wolfe, but Beckett's literary judgments may be less in question here than the importance he seems to attach to the quotations.

*   *   *

The first direct literary allusion Winnie makes is to *Hamlet:* "woe woe is me ... to see what I see" (10). It is a reference to Ophelia's recognition of Hamlet's madness, his deterioration: "O, what a noble mind is here o'erthrown! . . . O, woe is me, to have seen what I have seen, see what I see" (*Hamlet*, III, i). The reference was added late in the play's development in a verso note to the fifth full version of the play (H-3, p. 163), and provides the core of a curious and parodic comparison. Hamlet was virtually immobilized by his problems. He would have preferred not to act, to crawl instead into a cave and enjoy Willie's "Belacqua bliss." Winnie buried in her problem, Time, and Willie immobilized are versions of a contemporary Hamlet, who himself might have uttered Winnie's line, "What a curse, mobility!" (46). And Willie, like Hamlet, has also been unable to take his own life; as Winnie recalls: "Remember Brownie, Willie? . . . Remember how you used to keep on at me to take it away from you? Take it away, Winnie, take it away, before I put myself out of my misery" (33). This reference to Willie's suicide temptation is also added very late in the play's composition to provide a balance and foreshadowing for Willie's final struggle toward the revolver. The reference to Willie's suicidal tendency appears as the final note in the *ETE 56* notebook and is not included in the text until the third typescript, and then as an autograph revision.

For Hamlet, order and stability have collapsed, but the collapse is temporary. In Hamlet's world human action still mattered; it affected the events of men. Willie and Winnie's chaos is permanent, and Beckett's two immobilized characters yearn for oblivion, but their actions are inconsequential. Winnie admires Willie's ability to sleep: "sleep for ever . . . marvellous gift . . . wish I had it" (10). The phrase echoes Hamlet's "To die: to sleep;/ No more; and by a sleep to say we end/ The Heartache and the thousand natural shocks/ That flesh is heir to" (*Hamlet*, III, i). Ironically, Winnie makes certain that Willie's sleep is only temporary: she wakes him at the opening of the play and keeps Brownie from him.

Moreover, Hamlet's "Oh that this too, too solid flesh would melt," is echoed twice by Winnie: "and wait for the day to come . . . the happy day to come when flesh melts at so many degrees" (18); and again, "Shall I myself not melt perhaps in the end, or burn, oh I do not mean necessarily burst into flames, no just little by little be charred to a black cinder, all this . . . visible flesh'' (38). And in another allusion to *Hamlet*, Winnie's inability to act is dramatized through the impossibility of singing when one desires: "How often I have said . . . Sing now, Winnie, sing your song . . . and did not. Could not . . . . No, like the thrush, or the bird of dawning . . ." (40). The allusion was included in the first full holograph, and Beckett identifies it specifically in his marginalia to TS.-4: "Some say that ever 'gainst that season comes/ Wherein our Savior's birth is celebrated,/ The bird of dawning singeth all night long;/ And then, they say . . . The nights are wholesome . . . ." (*Hamlet*, I, i). But Winnie's world contains no seasons, no night in which the bird might sing. And Marcellus's remark suggests that the bird's song is a signal of the celebration of the birth, the coming of the savior and the withdrawal of the restless shades. Winnie's inability to sing is then appropriate. The savior is not coming; in fact the reference to the bird of dawning is followed by Winnie's strange feeling that someone is watching her, i.e., the ghosts are abroad. When she finally does sing, at the end of the play, Willie is struggling toward the revolver, in a parody, a travesty of salvation which itself fails. If Willie is in any way a savior, he is like Mr. Rooney in *All That Fall*, who saved the little boy from life by pushing him from a moving train. Mr. Rooney, however, seems to have succeeded in his role as savior. Willie not. And finally, Winnie's "I call to the eye of the mind," suggests Hamlet's vision of his father, "In my mind's eye, Horatio." While the last quotation does call to mind *Hamlet*, Beckett identifies it as a reference to the opening song of Yeats's "At the Hawk's Well."

Winnie then, at the very beginning of the play echoing Ophelia, calls our attention to the deterioration of a man, of men, once noble. Vestiges persist. Willie defines hog, clears up a grammatical point about hair, identifies the emmet's eggs. These are chivalrous touches like returning the parasol which slipped from Winnie's grasp early in the play. Willie was evidently once a great admirer of Winnie, and, if we use the admittedly slight evidence of his moustache as a link, Willie is Mr. Johnson, or Johnston, or Johnstone, who, as Winnie described him, had a "very bushy moustache." In Beckett's revision of the Johnston episode, moreover, he was careful to retain the reference to the moustache (see Chapter IV), but others were cut, again perhaps to vaguen the relationship. In the early version of the episode, Winnie reveals that Johnston's moustache "vanquished my scruples" (H-1). In the same version Winnie complains about being tired of the sight of the revolver. Willie mistakenly thinks Winnie is referring to him. She allays his fears as follows: "Oh not you, Edward, not you, who could ever weary of the sight of you . . . Your moustache alone . . ." (TS.-1, p. 11). And at one time Beckett contemplated making Willie's moustache much more conspicuous than it finally is: "B moustache visible on both sides of head" (*ETE 56*, p. 40). At the end of the play, when we finally see Willie full-face, we note he wears a " *Very long bushy white Battle of Britain moustache "* which he then proceeds to smooth like a villain of melodrama threatening the innocent, defenseless heroine (61).

Happy Days, in short, abounds with echoes of *Hamlet.* We see perhaps that the Prince's struggle against state and self has in the long run been futile; the forces of chaos and disorder have been winning, have indeed won. The ideals of the Renaissance, its hopes for art and science, its faith in man himself, ideals ushered in with Dante's *dolce stil nuovo* and developed by Shakespeare, have for modern man "become a weary decadence," useless and futile, as ineffective an aid to man as the Christianity suggested by Winnie's early prayers.

Winnie's next two quotations focus on her vanity. As she is concerned with her lips, she quotes Milton: "O fleeting joys/ Of Paradise, dear bought with lasting woes" (*Paradise Lost,* X, 741-742). The allusion to the misery of existence is obvious, and Beckett used the quotation as a replacement for his earlier thought to represent "the transitoriness of all things" with a Biblical allusion. Shortly thereafter, Winnie quotes Romeo as he discovered the drugged Juliet: "Ensign crimson . . . . Pale flag" (15). During the rehearsals of *Glückliche Tage,* Beckett told his actors that "Ensign crimson" is life, and "Pale flag," death.[14] Of course Juliet too is entombed at this point, and like Winnie, buried *alive* in a state between life and death. And as Romeo reminds us in this speech, "How oft when men are at the point of death/ Have they been merry!" (V,iii). *Romeo and Juliet* details a frustrated love, a love destroyed at least in part by forces beyond man, by something innocently called circumstance. As Shakespeare informs us in the prologue, these are "A pair of star-cross'd lovers." The failure of love is evident throughout *Happy Days,* but especially in Winnie's unconscious parody of the marriage vows which omits all reference to love: "I would obey you instantly, as I have always done, honoured and obeyed" (36). As the echoes of Shakespeare's tragedy reverberate through *Happy Days,* we are reminded that a consistent pattern of disaster runs through the affairs of men. Winnie's next quotation provides a variation on the love theme; this from Shakespeare's romance, *Cymbeline,* part of a funeral dirge sung by Imogen's lost brothers who believe Imogen is dead. She, like Juliet, is also drugged. While the end for Imogen and her husband, Posthumus Leonatus, is happier than Romeo and Juliet's, the bulk of *Cymbeline* recounts a love frustrated by sinister forces.

Thomas Gray's use of landscape to set the mood of a poem, his brooding on death and sorrow make him a particularly apt poet for Beckett (and Winnie) to quote, and her "laughing wild amid severest woe" (31) is an allusion to Gray's "Ode on a Distant Prospect of Eton College": "And moody Madness laughing wild/Amid severest woe." Gray's longing is for the innocence and ignorance of youth: "Alas regardless of their doom,/ The little victims play!/ No sense have they of ills to come,/ Nor care beyond today." The lines approach Beckett's description of Winnie's conception of Time, her existence only in the present: "Her time experience incomprehensible transport from one inextricable present to the next, those past unremembered, those to come inconceivable" (*Regiebuch*, p. 62). It is a child's sense of time. The present moment was and will be. "And should one day the earth cover my breasts, then I shall never have seen my breasts . . ." (38).

The entire mood of Gray's "Ode" reflects Beckett's view of tragedy, virtually a synonym for human existence, life: "To each his suffering: all are men,/ Condemned alike to groan." And Gray's solution to the oppression of knowing, understanding, seeing, is also Winnie's: "Thought would destroy their paradise./ No more; where ignorance is bliss/ 'Tis folly to be wise." It is *Ecclesiastes* again: "For in much wisdom is much grief: and he that increaseth knowledge increaseth sorrow" (1:18).

The mood suggested by Winnie's allusions then abruptly shifts as she evokes another vision of paradise, this time from Edward FitzGerald's translation of *The Rubáiyát of Omar Khayyám*. Though virtually unnoticed at the time of its publication, FitzGerald's translation of the Persian mathematician and astronomer's epigramatic collection of poems gained a tremendous popularity among the late Victorians. It appealed to a growing Epicurean revival, a reaction from the dour Victorian gospel of work. The poem suggests as an alternative to the oppression of social striving, a decadent hedonism. It is also another echo of the theme Beckett suggested in an earlier version of *Happy Days*, "the transitoriness of all things." "The Worldly Hope men set their Hearts upon/ Turns Ashes—or it prospers; and anon,/ Like Snow upon the Desert's dusty Face,/ Lighting a little hour or two—is gone" (*Rubáiyát*, 16). The theme is again close to *Ecclesiastes:* "How dieth the wise man? as the fool."

The *Rubáiyát* suggests that given man's transitory state, given the fact of deterioration, the most he can hope for is a temporary pleasure of the senses: "A Book of Verses underneath the Bough,/ A Jug of Wine, a Loaf of Bread—and Thou/ Beside me singing in the Wilderness—/ Oh, Wilderness were Paradise enow" (*Rubáiyát*, 12). Through the seven full versions of *Happy Days*, Beckett had used, either mistakenly or as an intentional misquotation, the line, "Happiness enow" (altered from "enough for my happiness" in the first holograph), changing it only in an autograph emendation in the fourth typescript to "Paradise enow." Evidently (and unfortunately) the typesetter missed the correction, as did Beckett reading proof, and the allusion was printed incorrectly in the first edition. It has subsequently been corrected and the allusion to the *Rubáiyát* clarified, the parody of Khayyám's idyllic vision sharpened. For Winnie is denied even this brief interlude of pleasure. She has no shade under a bough. The wilderness is within, and frightening—the lover's song, Willie's harsh, guttural response to the musicbox, a parody. If Winnie's plight had earlier served as a parody of Christian idealism and Renaissance humanism, it now parodies the Epicurean alternative—worldly pleasure.

The allusion to the *Rubáiyát* is followed quickly by Winnie's reference to Browning's "Paracelsus": "I say confusedly what comes uppermost" ("Paracelsus," *3.372*). The reference was evidently important to Beckett for he noted the quotation early in the *ETE 56* notebook, and, as with the FitzGerald quotation, Beckett's revisions clarify the reference. The earliest version of the Browning allusion made no specific reference to the poet. Browning's name was first included in the H-2 version to help the reader identify the allusion and establish the ironies surrounding the confusion of the poet with what is perhaps the brand name of the revolver and even, perhaps, the benevolent, elfin spirits. The quotation suggests not only the possible failure of gravity (an occurrence as unnatural as Paracelsus's rejection of love), a theme which Winnie develops shortly thereafter, but also the failure of human love. Paracelsus not only rejected authority and the traditional means of learning, but also human love in his pursuit of knowledge. He had none of Aprile's sensitivity toward people, art, and nature.

An additional irony, whether intentional or not, results from the close coupling of FitzGerald and Browning, especially when one of the themes connecting the allusions is the failure of love. On the death of Mrs. Browning, FitzGerald had written a friend, "Mrs. Browning's death is rather a relief to me, I must say: no more *Aurora Leighs,* thank God!" Needless to say, Browning's response in "To Edward FitzGerald" was bitter.[15]

Act II opens with a reference to Milton: "Hail, holy light" (*Paradise Lost,* III,1). The quotation continues the light-shade imagery; as Milton reminds us, "God is light," and light is eternal: "never but in the unapproachèd light/ Dwelt from eternity." But the celebration of the eternity of light is a sharp contrast to the reality of Winnie's condition. What Winnie needs, in point of fact, is not a rhapsody on the divinity of light, but shade, a relief from oppressive reality. The disjunction between the ideal and real is further developed in the next allusion to Keats's "Ode to a Nightingale," "beechen green." The song of the nightingale is an intoxicant which draws Keats's narrator from the woe of reality to the ideal of the imagination, but within the poem the narrator himself recognizes the disjunction, and the portion of the poem Winnie quotes refers to the idyllic abode of the bird which contrasts sharply to her own environment. The bird sings in the shade; Winnie is forced to suffer in the sun.

The Keats quotation re-sounds earlier images and themes. As with other allusions, Beckett clarified the Keats reference in revision. The earliest appearance (H-2, p. 137) was simply a reference to "Shade." The revision to "beechen green" not only sharpened the allusion to Keats, but strengthened the connection to Winnie's earlier amorous encounter, the Charlie Hunter episode, which also occurred "in the back garden at Borough Green, under the horse-beech" (15-16). And the horse-beech itself was revised from horse-chestnut. Also, the Johnston episode takes place in "The shadows deepening among the rafters" (16). Moreover, the nightingale is a thrush, the bird Winnie earlier coupled with "the bird of dawning." They would both signal the arrival of the savior, or at very least, salvation. The alternative to harsh reality is the idyllic grove of beechen green and the song of a bird reflecting a cosmic order, a celestial harmony, and perhaps an amorous interlude. But Winnie's world has only a parody of celestial music, Willie's spontaneous outburst. Nature is dead. She lives in the harsh light of day, in what Beckett has called in the *ETE 56* notebook "Eternal sun," and intimates that "tender is the night," and longs for "the wholesomeness of night." Finally, Keats's poem echoes the ignorance-is-bliss theme: "Where but to think is to be full of sorrow." Winnie picks up the theme soon after the Keats allusion: "not to know, not to know for sure, great mercy, all I ask" (51).

The Keats reference is followed shortly thereafter by an allusion to the Shakespearian comedy, *Twelfth Night*, an allusion added in an autograph revision to TS.-2. The title of Shakespeare's play alone resounds with ironies for Winnie. Twelfth Night is the night of the Epiphany, Christ's manifestation to the Magi. Winnie is Viola, yet disguised as Cesario, hinting of the strength of her love for the Duke: "She never told her love,/ But let concealment like a worm i'th'bud/ Feed on her damask cheek" (II, iv, 110-112). Viola's stoic restraint stands in sharp contrast to Winnie's ignorance, but Winnie too withholds her overt protestation of love until the very end of the play when she sings the Waltz Duet from *The Merry Widow*. The reunion of the lovers at the end of *Happy Days*, however, is a travesty of love. And Viola's image of grief is also appropriate for Winnie: "She sat like Patience on a monument,/ Smiling at grief" (II, iv, 114-115).

Winnie's reference to *Twelfth Night* contains another interesting dimension. Throughout Shakespeare's play runs an undercurrent of nostalgia for the good old days, for that merry old England represented by Sir Toby Belch, and in other Shakespearian plays by Falstaff. They are vestiges of medieval castle life now out of place, a nuisance in a Tudor country house. Winnie follows her *Twelfth Night* allusion with a recollection of her old style, an idyllic, romantic interlude: "The sunshade you gave me . . . that day . . . that day . . . the lake . . . the reeds" (53). The memory is for Winnie, as it was for Krapp, an ideal, a recollection of a time when retreat from the sun was possible. The word "sunshade" itself is a composite of the play's conflicting images, sun and shade. Part of Winnie's old style was the ability, the freedom, to withdraw from the oppressive sun: "I speak of when I was not yet caught—in this way—and had my legs and had the use of my legs, and could seek out a shady place, like you, when I was tired of the sun . . ." (38). Beckett himself took pains in his production to remove all shadows on the stage.[16]

The theme of love frustrated, the images of sun, song, shade, and change are further orchestrated in Winnie's allusion to a rather obscure Irish poet, Charles Wolfe. The allusion provides the only concrete suggestion we have of Winnie's ancestry: the poem is a minor, sentimental piece, one perhaps an

Irish schoolgirl might read as a student, "Go! Forget me." Winnie (mis)quotes the opening stanza:

> Go! forget me, why should sorrow
>   O'er that brow a shadow fling?
> Go! Forget me—and to-morrow
>   Brightly smile, and sweetly sing.
> Smile—though I shall not be near thee;
> Sing—though I shall never hear thee.
>   May thy soul with pleasure shine,
>   Lasting as the gloom of mine.

Hardly a classic. But her citing it as such reinforces our skepticism about Winnie's sensitivity and awareness. Willie is apparently gone. The quotation is Winnie's sentimental, self-pitying farewell to Willie, who now will never hear her sing. Ironically, the departure of the lover in Wolfe's poem brings on the night, but even this consequence of the failure of love is denied Winnie.

Almost immediately after the Wolfe quotation, Winnie begins a play within a play, complete with dialogue: the Shower-Cooker story again. Winnie opens the play in the manner of another Irishman, Yeats. The allusion is to the opening of "At the Hawk's Well" and is sung: "I call to the eye of the mind." It is another attempt to escape reality via the imagination. Yeats invites the audience's imagination to supply the props and scenery for the play, as well as some of the preliminary action, a man climbing a hill. The man climbing the hill will shortly be Willie. Perhaps we have crossed the line between reality and imagination. Perhaps Winnie created Willie climbing toward her, dressed in the old style. Winnie's savior may be a figment of her imagination.

The allusion to Yeats re-emphasizes the disjunction between the ideal and the real which is the core of Hamlet's problem as well as that of Keats's narrator. Yeats's life-long pursuit of universal order, of harmony between the imagination and reality, a harmony epitomized by the dancer in whose image artist and work of art fuse, serves as an ironic contrast to the disjunction, permanent and irreparable, between Winnie and Willie. Even the Unnamable comes closer to Yeatsian harmony than this couple: ". . . I still the teller and the told" (*Three Novels*, p. 310).

Winnie's final direct literary allusion is to Robert Herrick's "To the Virgins, to Make Much of Time," a poem also alluded to by the Unnamable: "For me to gather while I may" (*Three Novels*, p. 350). As Willie reappears Winnie asks, "Where are the flowers?" The pattern of Beckett's revisions of the Herrick quotation differs from the others. The earlier version was closer to Herrick's "Gather ye rosebuds while ye may." Earlier Winnie said, "All you need now is the rose in your button-hole" (H-2, p. 154). The final allusion to flowers is vaguer and would have been difficult to identify, if not impossible, had Beckett himself not done so in TS.-4. With the allusion clear, however, the image of Willie's coming to gather his rosebud is grotesquely comic, as well as another example of Winnie's incorrect assessment of Willie's quest.

Other of Herrick's images parallel the pattern Beckett established in *Happy Days*. Herrick's time "a-flying" and "The glorious lamp of heaven, the sun" again serve as ironic contrasts to Winnie's plight, where youth is lost and time has virtually ceased. Herrick could, after all, take "Delight in Disorder." His solution to the transitoriness of youth is similar to that in the *Rubáiyát*, a hedonistic solution impossible for Winnie, who "having lost but once her prime, . . . may forever tarry." Forever!

* * *

As the literary allusions build over the course of the play, as they echo each other, as images are repeated and gain an accumulated weight, we realize that the imaginative treatment of life (the province traditionally of literature), the order and hopes of literature are as mythologically unreal, as irrelevant to the human condition as the elaborate structure of divine, cosmic order devised by the Greeks. The hope provided by literature and the imagination is unfounded, a hope irreconcilable with reality. Literary and humanistic failure parallel the failure of religion to meet the needs of man. And although the Biblical allusions in *Happy Days* are not identified by Beckett or signaled by Winnie, they nonetheless saturate the play. In addition to using echoes of *Ecclesiastes*, the parody of Christ's "When two are gathered in my name," the ridicule of *Genesis* around which Beckett built the slight "Breath" and also used in *Happy Days* (i.e., "the nostrils . . . breath of life," 52), Beckett suggests parallels to Psalm 40 in *Happy Days*. The opening of the Psalm, in fact, provided the central situation for *Godot* some twelve years earlier:

> I waited patiently for the Lord; and he inclined unto me, and heard my cry. He brought me up also out of an horrible pit, out of the miry clay, and set my feet upon a rock, and established my goings. And he hath put a new song in my mouth . . . . Withhold not thou thy tender mercies from me, O Lord; let thy loving kindness and thy truth continually preserve me.
>
> (*Psalms*, 40: 1-3, 11)

And again, from the same Psalm which provided Beckett with the title for *All That Fall*: "The Lord is good to all: and his tender mercies are over all his works" (*Psalms*, 145: 9). And from *Isaiah*, the hope that the failure of mercy is only temporary:

> For the Lord hath called thee as a woman forsaken and grieved in spirit, and a wife of youth, when thou wast refused, saith thy God.
> For a small moment have I foresaken thee; but with great mercies will I gather thee. In a little wrath I hid my face from thee for a moment; but with everlasting kindness will I have mercy on thee, saith the Lord thy Redeemer.
>
> (*Isaiah*, 54: 6-8)

Of Beckett's early working titles, three, *Great Mercies, Tender Mercies, Many Mercies*, would have signaled the direct literary allusions; perhaps the signal would have been too strong for Beckett. Unlike Mr. and Mrs. Rooney who can laugh at the promise of the *Psalms*, Winnie continues to hope and believe as she sinks into her pit. While many of the literary works from which Winnie quotes focus on the failure of human love, the disjunction between the promise of the *Psalms* and Winnie's plight suggests something of the failure of divine love. Each quotation marches past Winnie as the Unnamable's characters, his lies, march before him, and each quotation is ridiculed by the desperation of Winnie's plight. But the audience sees the ridicule, not Winnie. The dramatic irony is intense in *Happy Days* precisely because Winnie retains her optimism, her faith, and is unaware of the contrast between the way in which things are and the way in which she thinks they are.

The pattern of literary allusions and echoes in *Happy Days* is complex. The themes of the failure of love, the misery of the human condition, the transitoriness of all things, the disjunction between the real and ideal, the misery of awareness, have been carefully reinforced in Winnie's literary allusions and reverberate throughout the play like a constant drumbeat. The word "mercy" itself becomes a refrain, like "happy." And in Beckett's selection of quotations and obliquer references virtually every historical epoch is represented: pre-Christian Greek philosophies, the blind religiosity and Christian Idealism of the Middle Ages, Renaissance Humanism, eighteenth century Rationalism, and nineteenth century Romanticism. The philosophies, literature, and religion of western man comprise the fragmented mythology against which Winnie fails and suffers, and like a jeweler's foil, mythology highlights the suffering.

References

1. Colin Duckworth, *Angels of Darkness* (New York: Barnes & Noble, Inc., 1972), p. 18.

2. Maria Jolas, "A Bloomlein for Sam," *Beckett at 60: A Festschrift* (London: Calder and Boyars, 1967), p. 16.

3. Harold Hobson, "Samuel Beckett: Dramatist of the Year," *International Theatre Annual, No. 1* (New York: The Citadel Press, 1956), p. 153.

4. Hugh Kenner, *Samuel Beckett: A Critical Study*, 2nd edition (Berkeley: University of California Press, 1968), p. 63. See also pp. 67-70, *et passim*.

5. See especially David H. Hesla, *The Shape of Chaos: An Interpretation of the Art of Samuel Beckett* (Minneapolis: University of Minnesota Press, 1971).

6. T. S. Eliot, "Myth and Literary Classicism," *The Modern Tradition*, ed. Richard Ellmann and Charles Feidelson, Jr. (New York: Oxford University Press, 1965), 681.

7. Richard Ellmann, *James Joyce* (New York: Oxford University Press, 1959), p. 715.

8. "Poetry is Vertical," *Transition*, 21 (March 1932), 148-149. The manifesto is signed by: Hans Arp, Samuel Beckett, Carl Einstein, Eugene Jolas, Thomas McGreevy, Georges Pelorson, Theo Rutra, James J. Sweeney, Ronald Symond.

9. Lawrence E. Harvey, *Samuel Beckett: Poet & Critic* (Princeton, N. J.: Princeton University Press, 1970), p. 423.

10. Ruby Cohn, *Samuel Beckett: The Comic Gamut* (New Brunswick: Rutgers University Press, 1962), pp. 252-255.

11. Hassan, p. 196.

12. John Fletcher, "The Arrival of *Godot*," *The Modern Language Review*, 64 (January 1969), 38.

13. Cohn, pp. 255-256.

14. Ruby Cohn, "Beckett Directs *Happy Days*," *Performance*, 1, No. 2 (April 1972), 115.

15. *The Norton Anthology of English Literature*, II, ed. M. H. Abrams et al. (New York: W. W. Norton & Co., 1968), p. 1007n.

16. Ruby Cohn, "Beckett Directs *Happy Days*," p. 117.

Appendix A

Character Names

	Male	*Female*
ETE 56: text:	Tom	W
notes:	"Not Edward Willie"	"Not Mildred Winnie"
H-1:	Tom pp. 1-11 B pp. 12-25 Ed pp. 25-28 Hubert pp. 28-33 Edward pp. 34-72	W pp. 1-39 M pp. 40-72
TS. -1, Act I:	Bee pp. 1-3 B pp. 3-7 Edward pp. 8-18 Willie p. 11, 18 (autograph)	W pp. 1-15 Mildred pp. 15-18 Winnie p. 18 (autograph)
H-2, Act I:	Tom p. 74 Willie pp. 74-132	Winnie pp. 74-132
TS.-1, Act II:	Willie throughout	Winnie throughout

Appendix B

Literary Allusions Identified by Beckett

Happy Days	Quotation	Stage added
1. what are those wonderful lines...woe woe is me ...to see what I see (10)	O, woe is me, T' have seen what I have seen, see what I see! (Ophelia, *Hamlet*, III, i)	H-3, p. 163; verso revision
2. What is that wonderful line?...Oh fleeting joys...oh something lasting woe. (14)	O fleeting joys of Paradise, dear bought with such lasting woes. (*Paradise Lost*, X, 741-742)	H-2, p. 80
3. Ensign crimson....Pale flag. (15)	beauty's ensign yet Is crimson in thy lips and in thy cheeks, And death's pale flag is not advanced there. (Romeo, *Romeo and Juliet*, V, iii)	H-2, p. 82; written out, H-3, p. 169
4. Fear no more the heat o'the sun. (26)	Fear no more the heat o'th' sun, (Guiderius, *Cymbeline*, IV, ii)	H-1, p. 32
5. what is that wonderful line...laughing wild ...something something laughing wild amid severest woe. (31)	And moody Madness laughing wild Amid severest woe. ("Ode on a Distant Prospect of Eton College")	TS.-2, p. 10, autograph revision
6. paradise enow. (32)	A Book of Verses underneath the Bough, A Jug of Wine, a Loaf of Bread—and Thou Beside me singing in the Wilderness—Oh, Wilderness were Paradise enow! (*The Rubáiyát of Omar Khayyám*)	Happiness enow in H-1, p. 42
7. Ever uppermost, like Browning. (33)	I say confusedly what comes uppermost; But there are times when patience proves a fault As now: This morning's strage encounter—you Beside me once again! (*Paracelsus*, III, 372-373)	H-1, p. 46

Appendix B

Continued

8. No, like the thrush or the bird of dawning, with no thought of benefit, to oneself or anyone else. (40)	Some say that ever gainst that season comes Wherein our Savior's birth is celebrated, This bird of dawning singeth all night long. (Marcelluss., *Hamlet*, I,i)	H-1, p. 58
9. Hail, holy light. (49)	Hail holy Light. (*Paradise Lost*, III, 1)	H-2, p. 134
10. Ah yes...then... now...beechen green (51)	That thou, light--winged Dryad of the trees, In some melodious plot Of beechen green, and shadows numberless, Singest of summer in full-throated ease. ("Ode to a Nightingale, 7-10)	"Shade," H-2, verso p. 137, 138. "beechen green," TS.-2, Act II, p. 2
11. *(eyes left, distends cheeks again)*...no ...no damask. (53)	She never told her love, But let concealment, like a worm i'the bud, Feed on her damask cheek. (Viola, *Twelfth Night*, II, iv)	TS.-2, Act II, p. 2; autograph revision
12. Go forget me why should something o'er that something shadow fling ...go forget me...why should sorrow...brightly smile...go forget me... never hear me...sweetly smile...brightly sing. (57)	Go, forget me! Why should sorrow O'er that brow a shadow fling? Go, forget me—and to-morrow Brightly smile and sweetly sing. Smile—though I shall not be near thee. Sing— though I shall never hear thee. May thy soul with pleasure shine, Lasting as the gloom of mine. ("Go! Forget me")	H-2, p. 148
*13. I call to the eye of the mind... (58)	I call to the eye of the mind ("At the Hawk's Well," 1)	H-2, p. 148
14. Where are the flowers? (61)	Gather ye rosebuds while ye may ("To the Virgins, to Make Much of Time")	"rose in your button hole," H-2, 154

* Not included among Beckett's notes in TS.-4, but is listed among the allusions Beckett sent to Alan Schneider and included in the list of allusions in the *Regiebuch*.

Appendix C

Collation: Typescript IV and First Edition

Act I	Typescript IV	First edition
12.1	*(brush)—it*	*brush—it*
12.22	*strikes*	*srikes*
18.1	*...hog's...(*	*...hog's (*
19.5	*puts them on*	*puts them on*
19.5	*No but this is just*	*No but this is just*
20.16	*the alternative.*	*the alternative?*
23.1	*Brush and comb it?*	*Brush and comb it?*
23.10	*Long pause.*	*Long pause.*
26.11	What. (*Pause.*) What?	What? (*Pause.*) What?
32.2	paradise enow.	happiness enow.
44.11	punctuates following.	punctuates following.)
48.21	Curtain	CURTAIN

Act II		
49.4	*moitonless*	*motionless*
52.9	(*Smile.*)	(*Smile*)
53.23	(*Smile.*)	(*Smile*)
54.26	(*Smile.*)	(*Smile*)
58.8	Mr	Mr.
58.17	he says.	he says
59.25	(*pause*)	(*pause.*)
63.19	Brrrum!	Brrum!
64.26	Curtain	CURTAIN

Appendix D

Collation of *Happy Days*, Printed Versions: 1st and 10th Printings

Page	First Printing	Tenth Printing
12.22	*srikes*	*strikes*
32.2	happiness enow.	paradise enow.
39.24-39.25	*The Merry Widow*	The Merry Widow

SELECTED BIBLIOGRAPHY OF CRITICISM

Abbott, H. Porter. *The Fiction of Samuel Beckett: Form and Effect.* Berkeley, 1973.

Admussen, Richard L. "The Manuscripts of Beckett's *Play*," *Modern Drama,* 16 (June 1973), 23-27.

Alpaugh, David. "Negative Definition in Samuel Beckett's *Happy Days*," *Twentieth Century Literature,* 2, No. 4 (January 1966), 202-210.

Alvarez, A. *Samuel Beckett.* New York, 1973.

Barnard, G.C. *Samuel Beckett: A New Approach.* New York, 1970.

Bermel, Albert. "Beckett Without Metaphysics," *Performance,* 1, No. 2 (April 1972), 119-126.

Calder, John, ed. *Beckett at 60: A Festschrift.* London, 1967.

Calepins de Bibliographie. Ed. R.J. Davis, J.R. Bryer and M.J. Friedman, and P.C. Hoy, no. 2, Samuel Beckett. Paris, 1971.

Camus, Albert. *The Myth of Sisyphus and Other Essays,* trans. Justin O'Brien. New York, 1955.

Clurman, Harold. "*Happy Days*," *The Nation,* 201 (October 18, 1965), 258-259.

―――. "Theater," *The Nation,* 193 (October 7, 1961), 234-235.

Coe, Richard N. *Samuel Beckett.* New York, 1968.

Coetzee, J.M. "The Manuscript Revisions of Beckett's *Watt*," *Journal of Modern Literature,* 2 (November 1972), 472-480.

Cohn, Ruby, ed. *Perspective* (Samuel Beckett issue), 9 (Autumn 1959), 119-196.

―――. "Samuel Beckett Self-Translator," *PMLA,* 76 (December 1961), 613-621.

―――. "Plays and Players in the Plays of Samuel Beckett," *Yale French Studies,* 29 (Spring-Summer 1962), 43-48.

___. *Samuel Beckett: The Comic Gamut*. New Brunswick, N.J., 1962.

___. "Philosophical Fragments in the Works of Samuel Beckett," *Criticism: A Quarterly for Literature and the Arts*, 6 (Winter 1964), 33-43.

___, ed. *Samuel Beckett: A Collection of Criticism*. New York, 1975.

___, ed. *Modern Drama* (Samuel Beckett issue), 9 (December 1966), 237-346.

___. "The Beginning of *Endgame*," *Modern Drama*, 9 (December 1966), 319-323.

___, ed. *Casebook on 'Waiting for Godot.'* New York, 1967.

___. "Beckett Directs *Happy Days*," *Performance*, 1, No. 2 (April 1972), 111-118.

___. *Back to Beckett*. Princeton, 1973.

Driver, Tom. "Beckett by the Madeleine," *Columbia University Forum*, 4, No.3 (Summer 1961), 21-25.

Duckworth, Colin, ed. *En attendant Godot*. London, 1966.

___. *Angels of Darkness: Dramatic Effect in Samuel Beckett with Special Reference to Eugéne Ionesco*. New York, 1972.

Eastman, Richard M. "Samuel Beckett and *Happy Days*," *Modern Drama*, 6 (February 1964), 417-424.

Ellmann, Richard. *James Joyce*. New York, 1959.

Esprit Créateur, l', 11, No. 3 (Fall 1971), 3-78.

Esslin, Martin. *The Theatre of the Absurd*. New York, 1961.

___, ed. *Samuel Beckett: A Collection of Critical Essays*. Englewood Cliffs, N.J., 1965.

Federman, Raymond. *Journey to Chaos: Samuel Beckett's Early Fiction*. Berkeley, 1965.

___, and John Fletcher. *Samuel Beckett: His Works and His Critics*. Berkeley, 1970.

Fletcher, John. *Samuel Beckett's Art*. New York, 1967.

———. "The Arrival of *Godot*," *The Modern Language Review*, 64, No. 1 (January 1969), 37.

———. *The Novels of Samuel Beckett*, 2nd ed. New York, 1970.

———, and Beryl S. Fletcher, eds. *Fin de Partie*. London, 1970.

———, and John Spurling. *Beckett: A Study of His Plays*. New York, 1972.

Friedman, Melvin J., ed. *Samuel Beckett Now*. Chicago, 1970.

———. "Samuel Beckett and His Critics Enter the 1970s," *Studies in the Novel*, 5, No. 3 (Fall 1973), 383-399.

Gilman, Richard. "The Stage: Beckett's *Happy Days*," *Commonweal*, 75 (October 13, 1961), 69-70.

Guicharnaud, Jacques, and June Beckelman. *Modern French Theatre from Giraudoux to Beckett*. New Haven, 1961.

Harvey, Lawrence E. *Samuel Beckett Poet & Critic*. Princeton, 1970.

Hassan, Ihab. *The Literature of Silence: Henry Miller and Samuel Beckett*. New York, 1967.

Hayman, David, ed. *James Joyce Quarterly* (Samuel Beckett issue), 8, No. 4 (Summer 1971).

Herring, Phillip F., ed. *Joyce's 'Ulysses' Notesheets in The British Museum*. Charlottesville, 1972.

Hesla, David H. *The Shape of Chaos: An Interpretation of the Art of Samuel Beckett*. Minneapolis, 1971.

Hobson, Harold. "Samuel Beckett: Dramatist of the Year," *International Theatre Annual, No. 1*. New York, 1956.

Hoffman, Frederick J. *Samuel Beckett: The Language of Self*. New York, 1964.

Janvier, Ludovic. *Pour Samuel Beckett*. Paris, 1966.

Kennedy, Sighle. *Murphy's Bed: A Study of Real Sources and Sur-real Associations in Samuel Beckett's First Novel*. Lewisburg, 1971.

Kenner, Hugh. *Samuel Beckett: A Critical Study*. Berkeley, 1967.

___. *A Reader's Guide to Samuel Beckett*. New York, 1973.

Kern, Edith. "Beckett's Knight of Infinite Resignation," *Yale French Studies*, 29 (Spring-Summer 1962), 49-56.

___. "Beckett and the Spirit of the Commedia Dell'Arte," *Modern Drama*, 9 (December 1966), 260-267.

___. *Existential Thought and Fictional Technique: Kierkegaard, Sartre, Beckett*. New Haven, 1970.

Knowlson, James, ed. *Samuel Beckett: an exhibition*. London, 1971.

___. *Light and Darkness in the Theatre of Samuel Beckett*. London, 1972.

Kott, Jan. *Shakespeare Our Contemporary*. New York, 1966.

___. *Theatre Notebook 1947-1967*. New York, 1968.

Leventhal, A. J. "The Beckett Hero," *Critique: Studies in Modern Fiction*, 7 (Winter 1964-65), 18-35.

Madtes, Richard E. "Joyce and the Building of Ithaca," *ELH*, 31 (December 1964), 443-459.

Mays, James. "Samuel Beckett Bibliography: Comments and Corrections," *Irish University Review*, 2 (Autumn 1972), 189-207.

Metman, Eva. "Reflections on Samuel Beckett's Plays," *Journal of Analytical Psychology*, 5 (January 1960), 41-63.

Morse, J. Mitchell. "The Ideal Core of the Onion: Samuel Beckett's Criticism," *French Review*, 38 (October 1964), 23-29.

Murray, Samuel. *The Tragic Comedian: A Study of Samuel Beckett*. Cork, 1970.

New Theatre Magazine: Samuel Beckett Issue. 11, No. 3.

O'Hara, J.D., ed. *Twentieth Century Interpretations of "Molloy," "Malone Dies," "The Unnamable."* New Jersey, 1970.

Peake, Charles. "*Waiting for Godot* and the Conventions of the Drama," *Prompt*, 4 (1964), 19-23.

Reid, Alec. *All I Can Manage, More Than I Could: An Approach to the Plays of Samuel Beckett.* New York, 1971.

Robinson, Michael. *The Long Sonata of the Dead: A Study of Samuel Beckett.* New York, 1969.

Schneider, Alan. "Reality is not Enough," (An interview with Richard Schechner), *Tulane Drama Review,* 9 (Spring 1965), 118-152.

Shenker, Israel. "A Portrait of Samuel Beckett, Author of the Puzzling *Waiting for Godot,*" *New York Times,* May 6, 1956, Section 2, pp. 1,3.

Trussler, Simon. *"Happy Days:* two productions and a text," *Prompt,* 4 (1964), 23-25.

Webb, Eugene. *The Plays of Samuel Beckett.* Seattle, 1972.

———. *Samuel Beckett: A Study of His Novels.* Seattle, n.d.

Worth, Katharine, ed. *Beckett the Shape Changer.* London, 1975.

Index

Admussen, Richard, 36, 43
Augustine, St., 4, 59
Beckett, Samuel
  (*works*)
  "Act Without Words, I," 18, 19, 38, 61
  "Act Without Words, II," 61
  All That Fall, 66, 72
  "Breath," 61
  Dream of Fair to Middling Women, 2
  Echo's Bones, 2
  Eleutheria, 2
  Endgame (Fin de Partie), 9, 12, 22, 23, 40, 43, 47, 48, 56
  Film, 43, 55
  Glückliche Tage, 7, 14
  Krapp's Last Tape, 49, 55
  "La Fin," 2
  Mercier et Camier, 2
  Molloy, 2, 60
  More Pricks Than Kicks, 2
  Murphy, 1, 2, 23, 24, 28
  Nouvelles et Textes pour rien, 2
  Play, 22, 38, 43
  Proust, 1, 2, 4, 17, 19-22, 33, 39, 44
  "Suite," 2
  The Unnamable, 24-25
  Waiting For Godot (En Attendant Gotot), 2, 12, 21, 22, 23, 33, 47-48, 55, 59
  Watt, 1, 11, 18
  "Words and Music," 7
Browning, Robert, 69

Camus, Albert, 19, 25
Coat, Tal, 44
Coe, Richard, 18
Cohn, Ruby, 43, 51, 52, 53, 56, 62, 63
Crane, Hart, 62

Dante, 62, 63, 67
Defoe, Daniel, 60
Descartes, René, 28, 52
Duckworth, Colin, 2, 3, 36

Eliot, T. S., 60, 61, 62

FitzGerald, Edward, 63, 68, 69
Flaubert, Gustave, 3
Fletcher, John, 2, 3, 63

Gray, Thomas, 67, 68

Harvey, Lawrence, 2, 62
Hassan, Ihab, 18, 63
Herrick, Robert, 71-72
Herring, Phillip, 2
Hobson, Harold, 4

Ionesco, Eugéne, 47

Jolas, Marie, 59
Joyce, James, 3, 22, 43, 52, 59, 60, 61
  (*works*)
  Ulysses, 2, 10, 60, 61
  Work in Progress, 3, 60

Keats, John, 63-64, 65, 69-70, 71
Kenner, Hugh, 60
Kern, Edith, 29
Kierkegaard, Sören, 29
Knowlson, James, 36, 49
Kott, Jan, 38, 39

Merry Widow, The, 13, 63, 70
Milton, John, 26, 61, 65, 67, 69

O'Hara, J. D., 3, 4

Parmenides, 24
Pythagoras, 60

Richardson, Samuel, 60
Robinson, Michael, 55

Sartre, Jean-Paul, 60
Schneider, Alan, 7, 11, 13, 28, 63
Shakespeare, William, 63, 65, 67, 70
  (*works*)
  Cymbeline, 43, 53, 62, 67
  Hamlet, 27, 65-66
  King Lear, 42
  Romeo and Juliet, 67
  Twelfth Night, 63, 70
Sisyphus, 61
Swift, Jonathan, 47

Tantalus, 61

Velde, Bram van, 41
Verticalism, 61

Watt, Isaac, 43
Weston, Jessie 62
Wittgenstein, Ludwig, 60
Wolfe, Charles, 64-65, 70-71
Wordsworth, William, 1

Yeats, William B., 65, 66, 71

Zeno, 24, 60

www.ingramcontent.com/pod-product-compliance
Lightning Source LLC
Chambersburg PA
CBHW030147240426
43672CB00005B/310